Consequences

50 SHORT STORIES FOR ASSEMBLIES

Written by

Rod Brockway

First published
January 04 in Great Britain by

Educational Printing Services Limited
Albion Mill, Water Street, Great Harwood, Blackburn BB6 7QR
Telephone: (01254) 882080 Fax: (01254) 882010
e-mail: enquiries@eprint.co.uk web site: www.eprint.co.uk

ISBN 1 904374 61 1

'Consequences'

A further delightful collection of Rod Brockway's thought-provoking stories.

This valuable new resource for assemblies addresses a comprehensive range of issues with great sensitivity.

The material may be photocopied for use in classrooms, for group reading activities and for use in delivering moral and social education.

The author, Rod Brockway, started his teaching career in the Falkland Islands. He was a Primary School Headteacher for 15 years and is now a Creative Writing tutor for the Open College of the Arts.

'Consequences' is Rod's second book for assemblies. 'Would You Believe It?' - an equally fascinating collection of stories - is also available from Educational Printing Services Limited.

Neither book can fail to inspire children and stimulate discussion.

Contents:

When a duck asked for help, Ricky could hardly refuse!

Ducknapped

'I must be dreaming,' Ricky thought.

He was looking in the window of a sweet shop when, out of the corner of his eye, he noticed a duck hurrying up the street, quacking crossly to herself. She was followed by a line of tiny, chattering ducklings.

The duck paused, glanced round at them, then headed straight towards Ricky. She fixed her beady black eyes on him as she waddled closer.

When she stopped, the line of ducklings stopped too. They all turned their heads and stared anxiously back down the street.

'What are they waiting for?' Ricky wondered. Minutes ticked by but then, just as Ricky was about to walk away, two more tiny ducklings appeared.

'If a car comes now, they'll be flattened,' Ricky thought. 'They're so young, they can hardly control their feet.'

He looked in both directions. It was surprisingly quiet, considering it was a Saturday.

'Batman to the rescue!' he sighed. He sprinted over to them. What else could he do? The duck stood patiently at the open door of the sweet shop. She didn't seem to notice that her other ducklings had disappeared inside. She watched anxiously as Ricky picked the latecomers up and returned with them, gently cupped in his hands.

Suddenly the owner of the sweetshop poked her head out of the door. 'So you're the culprit are you? It's not funny letting the poor little things loose in the town. Take them back where they belong.'

Ricky tried to explain but she wouldn't listen. She stamped her foot as the confused little family scuttled past her.

Ricky glared at the duck. 'So what do I do?' he pleaded.

The duck gave a low quack and glared back.

A greengrocer came out of his shop on the other side of the road, chuckling to himself. 'Here's a box for them,' he said. 'Get them to the river. That's where they should be.' But the tiny creatures were now racing in all directions. 'You could do with some help,' he laughed.

For the next ten minutes, Ricky, the man – and the duck – chased after the excited ducklings.

The crowd of people who quickly gathered thought it was a huge joke. They all clapped when the ducklings were safe in the box.

As Ricky looked down at them, he felt like saying, 'You're nothing to do with me.' But he didn't. Instead, he carried them to the end of the street with Mrs Duck waddling behind him.

'Can't you go any faster?' he said, looking round at her. 'This is hopeless.'

At that moment he heard the sound of a bus behind him. Without thinking, he turned and waved his hand at it. It stopped and Ricky climbed on.

'Do you go to the bridge?' he asked.

The driver nodded.

'£1.40 return.' Then he looked down and his mouth fell open. Mrs Duck was there.

'This has to be a joke,' bellowed the driver. He pointed at the bewildered creature. 'Off!' he snapped fiercely.

An old lady rose from her seat. 'I'm shocked,' she said. 'You can't treat a passenger like that. Not even a duck.'

The driver was about to explode. 'A duck is not a passenger.'

'Why not?' she protested.

The driver thought hastily. 'Because it hasn't any money.'

'Are we going to sit here all day?' called a man from the back of the bus. 'I'll pay its fare. So what is it, single, for a duck and family, to the river?'

The driver scratched his head. 'Can't carry ducks, against regulations,' he muttered.

'Who cares about regulations?' said a woman clutching a bag of shopping. 'Just get going. It's late and my hubby wants his tea.'

The driver sighed deeply. 'There'll be hell to pay if an inspector sees this . . . All right. Sit down, hang on to that animal – and make sure there's no mess.' He put the bus into gear, the engine roared and away they went.

It only took a few minutes to reach the bridge. As the bus screeched to a halt, the duck waddled past the driver, hesitated for a moment and then jumped down onto the pavement.

One by one, Ricky placed her family beside her. They lined up before chasing after her as she marched down to the riverbank. On the bridge, Ricky watched them plunging happily into the water.

Home at last!

'I must get home too,' he thought. 'It's late and mum will be worried.' Laughing to himself, he turned and ran off.

Thought for the day:
Grown ups take care of children but it's the responsibility of all of us to care for creatures great and small.

Something to consider:
What can we do in our everyday lives to help look after animals?

Sometimes life gives us an opportunity to do something really important.

This is the story of a small girl who lived in Eastern Europe. She loved animals – and hated cruelty.

Elephant Girl

'Have you heard? A circus is coming,' said Mr Hasheck. 'Everyone's talking about it.'

'But why come here?' asked his wife. 'Of course we'd enjoy it, but who could buy a ticket? We're all far too poor.'

'No, they aren't coming to entertain,' said Mr Hasheck. 'They just want to rest for a week before moving on.'

He turned round as the kitchen door flung open. Claudia, a small girl with black, curly hair, rushed in.

'Dad, Mum . . . ' she said breathlessly. 'A circus has arrived. There's a huge tent and lots of caravans down in the valley. Can I go and see?'

Mrs Hasheck hesitated for a moment. 'Yes, I suppose so. But don't be too long. It'll soon be time for tea.'

Claudia grabbed her coat and dashed out of the house.

As she crossed the fields she could see an enormous red and white striped tent in the distance. She paused and gazed at it in wonder. It was bigger than she could ever have imagined.

Gasping with excitement, she ran towards it. A surly-looking man came to the entrance, sucking on a blade of grass. He threw a piece of meat to a dog, then waited as Claudia approached.

'Sorry,' he said. 'You can't come here. We're training animals. They could be dangerous.'

Claudia felt bitterly disappointed. 'It's not fair,' she thought. 'Nothing ever happens in our village.' She wandered gloomily away and the man disappeared back into the tent. 'Just a quick look,' she muttered. 'That's all I want. And why not?'

She should have followed the path back to the village. Instead, she followed the hedge towards the caravans parked on the far side of the field. It was very quiet. No one came out to challenge her as she slipped past.

Beyond the caravans were two rows of gigantic cages. Her heart began to pound. She couldn't see inside but there was loud scuffling and snuffling.

Towering above her was the tent. A section of the canvas wall was hanging open. She went over and cautiously peered in.

A pair of gigantic elephants were attempting - unsuccessfully - to balance on a log.

Beside them, a man was shouting and brandishing a long pole. He jabbed at them viciously, every time they failed.

Claudia watched in horror for a long time. She could not bear it any longer; she turned and ran. She didn't stop until she reached home, and was desperate to tell her Mum and Dad.

'Aren't you hungry?' asked Mum.

'No, not really,' said Claudia. She felt too sad to eat. 'How could he be so cruel?' she asked.

'It's terrible, isn't it?' said Dad. 'But the man must be an expert. There's nothing we can do. He must know what's best.'

'Best?' snapped Claudia as she stormed out of the room. 'There's no excuse.'

'By the way,' said Mum at bedtime. 'There's going to be a procession through the village tomorrow. There'll be clowns, acrobats, lions, tigers – and elephants! You'll enjoy that.'

Claudia didn't answer. 'I don't think so!' she thought.

The next afternoon everyone stood outside their houses chattering excitedly. 'They're coming,' someone shouted at last.

There they were, led by the ring master in a bright red jacket, all skipping, leaping and tumbling as they turned the corner and progressed down the road.

Claudia stood well back. She felt confused. Yes, it was the most colourful and exciting event she had ever seen. But she felt like crying as the two huge elephants lumbered past. There was such sadness in their eyes.

Suddenly there was shouting, cheering and clapping. A family of clowns were blowing horns and screaming as they threw custard pies.

The two elephants lurched sideways. A baby elephant, walking behind them, squealed with fear and, in a panic, rushed to the side of the road.

It was past Claudia in an instant. She watched as it disappeared into the darkness of her father's barn. Without thinking, she raced to the heavy wooden doors and slammed them.

She recognised the surly man hurrying towards her with a heavy pole. How could she forget him?

''Nothing to worry about,' he shouted. 'Just open the doors and leave it to me.'

Claudia was smouldering with fury. She shook her head.

He was a big man. He glared down at her. 'Don't be silly,' he said. 'Just stand aside.'

Claudia felt frightened but stood her ground. 'No,' she snapped angrily. 'I've seen how cruel you are.'

'Nonsense,' he said. 'You know nothing about it.'

'I think she does,' bellowed her Dad, arriving with all the villagers. 'No more cruelty!

No more cruelty!' chanted the crowd. 'Promise - or we keep the elephant and call the police,' someone shouted.

The man, looking very shaken, nodded quickly.
'All right Claudia,' her dad said quietly. 'Open the door.'

'What if he breaks his promise?' said Claudia that evening. 'How shall we know?'
'We shan't – but at least we've made him think,' said her Dad. 'Sometimes we just have to trust.'

Thought for the day:
We often see things that are wrong in the world and feel powerless to change them. That shouldn't stop us from trying.

Small actions sometimes have surprising results.

Something to consider:
Today, animals are treated more kindly than they used to be but they still need our protection.

Have you ever been to a circus or a zoo? What do you think about them?

Dave was a boy who believed he was useless. I wonder why!

Useless

Dave sat at the back of the class yawning. Mrs Palmer had been reading a story to the class – 'A Christmas Carol' - about mean old Scrooge, haunted by gruesome ghosts!

'Why don't we perform it at the Christmas party?' she suggested.

'Count me out,' Dave thought gloomily. 'I'm useless. I never get chosen for anything.'

Brian, a small but noisy boy, who was always calling out in lessons, leaned across to him. 'I bet I get a good part!' he said. Then he stuck his hand in the air and called out. 'Please, please Miss, can I be a ghost? I'll be really frightening!'

Mrs Palmer looked doubtful. 'We'll just have to wait and see,' she said.

Later, when Dave was walking home, he saw Brian in front of him. He was kicking a football against a fence. A small boy was standing nearby.

'For the last time, give it back. It's mine.'

'So? You'll have to be patient, won't you?'

The boy seemed close to tears. 'I'll tell my mum about you.'

Brian sniggered. 'You think I'm scared?'

'Can I have my ball . . . please?'

'O.K. Catch it then.' He kicked the ball over the fence and then ran off laughing.

The fence was very high. The boy searched for a cracked panel to peer through. Dave went over to him. 'Can you see it?' he asked.

'No, I can't... '

'Well I can,' said a gruff voice.

Dave and the boy looked up in surprise. A scruffy-looking man with a bushy, white beard was standing beside them. He was so tall, he could easily see over.

'There it is,' he said. 'Under that tree next to the house.'

Dave squinted through the crack. Sure enough, it was there, hidden in some long grass. Dave wanted to thank the stranger but he had already walked away.

'How can we get it?' pleaded the boy. 'It was my birthday present.'

'Don't worry. It's no problem,' said Dave. He stared at the fence thoughtfully. There was only one thing to do. He went to the front door of the house and knocked. After what seemed a very long time, it opened. A woman peered out.

'Yes? What do you want?' she asked.

'Our ball's gone in your garden. Can we get it please?'

'You kids cause nothing but trouble. You're all rude and noisy.'

Dave stared at her. He couldn't think what to say.

She sighed impatiently. 'All right, I suppose you'd better come through.'

Dave followed her silently to the garden door.

'Be careful,' she snapped. 'I don't want you trampling on anything.'

'I shan't,' said Dave. 'Look. It's just over there, under the tree.' He ran across and picked it up.

'I don't get a moment's peace,' the woman said.

Dave mumbled an apology as he left the house.

The door slammed behind him.

The boy was waiting on the pavement. 'Thanks Dave,' he said, and off he went clutching the ball tightly.

Dave wandered on along the pavement. He hadn't gone far when, in the distance, he saw someone sitting on a doorstep. 'It's the same man,' thought Dave as he got closer. 'I wonder why he's sitting there.'

'Thank you!' he called to the man as he hurried past.

The man didn't seem to hear. He was busy rummaging in a bag. Next to him was an assortment of money and a few sweets.

Dave felt sorry for him. He walked back and dropped 20p at the man's feet. Then he ran off home.

'I must be stupid,' he muttered. 'That was the last of my pocket money.'

The next morning, Dave was startled when Mrs Palmer walked into the classroom with a visitor. It was a man - a tall man with a beard.

'Him again? It can't be! Why would he come here?' Dave thought.

The man talked to Mrs Palmer for a few minutes. Then they both looked in Dave's direction. The man nodded.

'Children, this gentleman has been telling me about a boy he saw in the town.' She looked very hard at Dave.

He started to panic.

Brian sniggered. 'Dave's in trouble! What's he been up to then?'

'Yesterday,' the man said, 'I was decorating the kitchen and had to go out for more paint. When I arrived home I couldn't find my key. I sat on the doorstep and emptied my pockets. Eventually I found it in my shopping bag - exactly where I'd put it! I'm getting forgetful in my old age!' He glanced at Dave. 'But one thing I couldn't forget was the way you helped a small boy. I just had to tell your teacher. You deserve a reward!' The man suddenly laughed. 'By the way, I owe you 20p.' He was still laughing as he hurried from the room.

Dave felt bewildered.

He felt even more bewildered when Mrs Palmer chose him to be a ghost. At first he was excited.

'Yes! That'll be great,' he said. But then he thought doubtfully. 'Why me? I'm useless at everything.'

In fact, when they saw the play everyone, except Brian, agreed he was the most frighteningly gruesome ghost they had ever seen!

'He wasn't that good,' Brian snarled. 'I'd have been better.'

Thought for the day:

We all have something to offer others. It may be more valuable than money.

Something to consider:

Brian took a small boy's ball. He was a bully.

Perhaps bullies are cowards. What do you think?

This is the story of a small boy and a big bully!

The Threat

Laura had been given a kite for her birthday. It was in the shape of an eagle and was enormous.

'You'll need some help,' said her brother. 'I could go up to the field with you now.'

'OK,' she said. 'I'll tell mum.'

Five minutes later she was ready. 'Come on Ned. Don't waste time,' she called.

Still pulling on his coat, he followed her down the garden path and into the road. Laura glanced at the sky.

'It's good kite-flying weather,' she said. 'There's just the right amount of wind. It'll be great.'

But as soon as they ran into the field they knew there would be trouble. On the far side they could see a group of boys. They recognised one of them. A tall, aggressive boy called Sid. He was sitting on a bike that was far too small. Another boy was trying to pull him off.

'Just ignore him,' said Laura. 'Pretend we haven't seen him.'

Ned helped to unfold the kite. Then he held it as high as he could while his sister unwound the string. 'That's enough,' he called. 'Try it now.'

Moments later, the kite was soaring into the sky.

'Just look at it,' Laura shouted.

'Give it here,' snapped a voice behind her. 'I'll get it twice as high as that.'

She twisted round and gasped with dismay. It was Sid. He snatched the string from her and ran off laughing loudly. His friends stood by the hedge, whistling and cheering. Laura started to cry.

Sid was tugging violently at the string of her kite. Ned stood watching silently. Then, to his sister's amazement, he suddenly sprang forward.

'Wait here. I'll be back!' he shouted.

Laura had never seen him run so fast. He was only a small boy but he charged towards Sid bellowing like a bull.

'Stop! Stop now – or you're dead!'

Sid did stop. He stared in amazement. He couldn't believe what was happening. He held out the kite string as Ned approached.

'Here - have your stupid kite,' Sid muttered. 'But you wait. My gang will get you tomorrow.'

Ned's hand started to shake as he gently towed the kite back to his sister.

She looked very hard at him. She had never thought of him as tough and brave before.

'Thanks,' she said.

The next morning in assembly, the Headteacher had an important announcement to make.

'Yesterday afternoon,' he said, 'a man was walking his dog on a field near here. He saw a boy flying a kite too close to a high voltage electric cable. If another boy hadn't stopped him quickly, he would have been killed.'

From that day on, Sid has been a lot nicer to everyone. Especially Ned.

Thought for the day:
Bullies often pick on children smaller than themselves and don't consider the feelings of others.

What's your opinion?
Perhaps we'll never know why Ned chased Sid and told him to stop. Do you think it was simply to get his sister's kite back?

Some people don't consider the feelings of others.
Perhaps the boy in this story learned his lesson!

The Last Laugh

Alison sat on the beach licking her ice cream anxiously. She was expecting trouble. There was no reason for a crowd of boys to play so close. The beach stretched for miles and was almost deserted. Suddenly the most annoying of them, Gavin, a small boy with a laugh like a hyena, swung around and hurled a ball at her. It landed with such force that sand flew up in her face. When she could see again, there he was, grinning from ear to ear.

'Sorry,' he cackled.

A seagull was standing close by. He charged after it, shouting and throwing handfuls of sand.

Alison glared at her spoiled ice cream.

'Stupid boy!' growled her Dad. He heaved himself out of his deck chair, puffing angrily.

Gavin picked up the ball and was about to throw it again. But he hesitated.

Alison's dad was a big man. Very big. 'Why do you have to play here?' he bellowed. 'Just go away – all of you.'

The boys looked sheepish. 'Sorry,' one of them mumbled.

'Come on you lot,' shouted Gavin. 'What are you waiting for?' He was already running into the distance. Suddenly he turned and poked out his tongue.

Alison pretended not to notice.

'It's a pity about the ice cream,' said Mum calmly. 'Never mind. We've plenty of flapjack.'

Alison was still eating when the gull returned. It approached and balanced on one leg, staring at her. She threw a large crumb. The bird lunged forward and caught it easily. Then it found the remains of the ice cream lying in the sand. It jabbed at it hungrily with its large yellow beak. When there was none left it walked slowly back to Alison.

She was now busy drawing a picture. Alison couldn't help noticing the gull out of the corner of her eye, standing close beside her with its head on one side, watching every movement of her pencil.

As she placed the picture of a seagull on the sand she asked, 'There, what do you think of that?'

Her new friend stepped forward and pecked at it excitedly with his beak.

The next day was Saturday. As the tide went out, the beach became crowded. There was to be a sandcastle competition. The first prize: a flight over the bay in a helicopter. Of course, everyone wanted to win.

Alison was excited. She hurried onto the beach and started digging frantically.

'We'll leave you to get on with it,' Mum called from high on the sea wall.

Alison was far too busy to hear. But she couldn't help hearing when Gavin arrived with four of his noisy friends. Did they have to start digging that close to her? She glanced at them and fumed. Then she ignored them and carried on.

She was working slowly and carefully now, building towers, walls and even a fine bridge of sand across the moat. It was only when she had finished that she sat back.

To her surprise, she realised that her friendly gull had returned. How long it had been there, standing on one leg, she didn't know. With its head on one side, it was silently studying the neighbouring castle. It was amazingly tall. Gavin was stretching up to poke tiny windows in the highest towers. His friends had gathered round, cheering and jumping up and down. One of them stepped back heavily. Alison's castle was right behind him. She held her breath.

'Mind what you're doing!' she yelled.

He turned to her. 'You really think yours could win? I don't think so!'

'What a joke,' Gavin sneered. Then he suddenly screamed. 'Get off! Get off!' He lunged forward. The seagull, which had landed on his castle, sprang into the air.

As Gavin fell, the boys looked on in shocked silence. Their castle had collapsed. Gavin felt sick. He could see a helicopter approaching. And circling above the heads of the crowd was a seagull. It was laughing.

'Do be careful boys,' boomed a commanding voice. 'This isn't the place to fool around, is it?'

She was a large woman. A badge pinned to her coat said 'JUDGE'. In her arms was a silver cup.

'What have we here? Definitely the smallest entry in the competition.' She smiled at Alison. 'It's also, without doubt, the best!'

○ ○ ○ ○ ○ ○ ○ ○ ○

Thought for the day:

Seagulls can be a nuisance to us on the beach, but no creature should be badly treated. They might say that humans can be a nuisance too!

○ ○ ○ ○ ○ ○ ○ ○ ○

What's your opinion?

Does the story tell us that Gavin wasn't really sorry when sand ruined Alison's ice cream? Do you think Alison laughed when his castle collapsed? If she did, was she justified?

This is the story of a cat who enjoyed gobbling food that wasn't his!
In the end he got his just desert.

Jake's Last Stand

Jake was the terror of the town.

Not only was he a giant of a cat. He was grossly overfed, greedy and bad tempered. Of course, tiny creatures such as birds, mice and moles were frightened of him. But cats were too!

Especially Oliver, Mrs Pringle's Pedigree Persian who lived next door. At meal times, Jake, having already eaten more than some cats eat in a week, would squeeze through Oliver's cat-flap, push him roughly aside and gobble as much food as he fancied. Which meant that poor Oliver was always hungry – and in trouble if he asked for more.

One day Mrs Pringle had invited special guests for dinner. She was in the kitchen preparing a delicious plate of fresh salmon when there was a knock on the door. She hurried to answer it. By the time she returned, the fish had mysteriously disappeared. Except, that is, for a neatly bitten-off tail and mayonnaise paw prints across the floor.

'You thieving animal,' bellowed Mrs Pringle. 'Where are you?'

Opening one eye, Oliver peered out from a lavender bush in his favourite corner of the garden.

'Who me?' he thought anxiously. 'What have I done?'

His mistress threw open the back door. 'You good for nothing cat,' she shouted. The door slammed and there was silence. A few minutes later, Jake appeared.

'Been bad?' he smirked. He yawned and stretched his paw to wipe the last of the mayonnaise from behind his ear. He smacked his lips. 'Delicious,' he purred. 'Excellent. You really should try some.'

Oliver didn't answer. He was staring into the long grass behind Jake. Something was moving there. He thought very quickly.

Then he said, 'Jake, do you know what's behind you . . . ? I hope you're not frightened of dogs.'

A hint of fear passed across Jake's face. 'A dog? You think I'm scared?' He pretended to clean his whiskers as he glanced round. He couldn't see clearly but a creature was certainly there, hidden in the grass.

'I'd better be going,' he said. Trying hard to keep calm, he turned and walked away. When he thought he was out of sight, he ran.

That night Jake had a terrible nightmare. He was face to face with a huge, snarling hound - and what was worse, Oliver was there too - grinning as he gobbled Jake's food!

From then on, Jake, the terror of the town, kept right away from Oliver's house.

'It's not that I'm scared,' he said to himself. 'But it's silly to take risks, isn't it?'

Oliver lay in his favourite corner of the garden. He smiled to himself as his new friend played peacefully on the lawn.

'I never said you were a dog, did I?' he chuckled. 'If Jake knew he'd run away from a rabbit he'd be really angry.'

Thought for the day:
Although they wouldn't admit it, bullies are often cowards.

Something to consider:
Oliver may not have been big and strong – but he used his brain instead. How?

Philip hated going shopping.
His little sister made it even worse!

A Sweet Tale

Philip stuck his hands in his pockets and sighed.

'I hate supermarkets,' he thought, watching his little sister gloomily. Today she was even more annoying than usual.

As Mum inspected a packet of frozen sausages, Fiona flung her arms in the air, skipped and twirled like a drunken ballet dancer - and almost knocked over a shop assistant.

Philip pretended not to notice. He wandered over to the magazines and picked up a copy of 'Motorcycle Monthly.' He was gazing longingly at the pictures when, suddenly, he heard his mum's voice. She sounded annoyed.

'Please Fiona,' she snapped. 'Just stand still.'

As Philip replaced the magazine his little sister snatched a bag of crisps from a shelf and shook it excitedly.

'Cheese and onion flavour. Yum yum!' she said hungrily.

'No Fiona, put it back. We've plenty at home already,' Mum said.

'Choc chip ice cream?' asked Fiona hopefully.

'Philip,' Mum begged. 'Look after your sister while I do the shopping. Please?' she added desperately.

'Come on,' said Philip. 'We'll go and count sauce bottles. That'll be fun.'

Fiona hooted with laughter. 'Catch me first,' she called. Then she disappeared into a crowd of shoppers.

'Go after her quickly Philip,' implored Mum. 'Just keep her out of mischief for ten minutes.'

'Where's she gone?' Philip muttered. He couldn't see her anywhere. 'I know,' he thought. 'Sweets! That's where she'll be.'

He rushed through the store, past fresh baked bread, beans, bananas, broccoli . . . and there she was! Gazing at her favourite sweets, out of reach on the top shelf. As he hurried towards her, she put a foot on the bottom shelf, stretched up and started to climb. Philip's heart missed a beat. He gasped with horror.

'No,' he wailed. 'Don't do it.' He was too late.

With a sickening crash the entire row of shelves toppled forward. His little sister leaped out of the way. Everything hit the floor and sweets slid, bounced and rolled in all directions.

Fiona didn't say a word. Although surrounded by mouthwatering chocolate bars, she didn't touch them. She knew she was already in big, big trouble.

Suddenly there was a cry of anguish from the next aisle. Philip nearly choked with fear. 'What's happening now?' he thought. He picked his way through the debris and peered anxiously round the corner. A bewildered old man was sitting on the floor clutching a tube of extra strong mints.

'I put my foot on this,' he said shakily. 'I never was any good at roller skating.'

Philip took him by the arm and helped him up.

The store manager appeared. 'Are you all right sir?' he asked.

'I think so, thank you. I feel a little wobbly - but this young man was very helpful.'

The manager looked at Philip. 'You look wobbly too,' he said. 'Choose a packet of sweets. That'll make you feel better. I can't understand it. The shelves shouldn't have collapsed,' he muttered unhappily.

Philip felt a little hand grasp his. 'Sorry,' his little sister whispered tearfully. 'I didn't mean it.'

They found Mum at the check-out. She finished paying, then glanced at Fiona.

'You're very quiet, young lady. I hope you've been good.'

Fiona nodded.

'Everything O.K. Philip?'

He looked at his little sister and hesitated for a moment. 'Yes, everything's fine,' he answered. 'I just want to go home.'

Thought for the day:

Sometimes people can be very annoying. It's difficult always to act with patience and understanding.

What's your opinion?

If you were Philip, would you have told the store manager and your Mum what really happened? Should you always tell the truth?

The girl in this story felt frighteningly small.
She was desperate for help.

King of the Castle

'Where am I going?' wondered Yasmin. 'How much further? How far? How far?'

She stumbled on, her feet sinking into the seemingly endless sand. She screwed up her eyes against the blazing sun. She licked her parched lips.

'If only I could have a drink,' she thought as she followed the footprints. 'I'm so thirsty.'

Other footprints crossed from right to left. Feeling tired and confused, she flopped down and started to cry.

Not far away, on a huge mound, stood a castle.

Through her tears, Yasmin saw battlements and towers silhouetted against a clear blue sky. In the half-dug moat lay a bucket and spade.

The beach was quickly becoming crowded. Strangers in huge hats and brightly coloured clothes. Laughing and shouting, they passed her by. Her frightened screams grew louder and louder.

She felt so alone.

Becky and Paul were walking back from the sea when they heard her cries. They ran over.

'What's the matter?' Jenny asked.

But little Yasmin, tears streaming down her face, couldn't answer.

'She's obviously lost,' said Paul. 'So what do we do?'

Becky shrugged her shoulders. 'I don't know,' she said. 'The beach is packed with people. How can anyone hope to find her?'

'There's only one answer,' said her brother. 'She needs to be really high - where she can be seen.'

He looked up at the magnificent castle.

'No,' pleaded Becky. 'We can't put her there. It took hours to build. It'll be ruined.'

They both looked from the castle to the small, unhappy girl.

Becky sighed. 'O.K. then. Lift her up.'

Yasmin, suddenly swept high into the air, was too startled to protest. For a moment she sat in silence, gazing out over the crowded beach.

Then she started to point excitedly. A man and woman, looking very worried, were close by.

'Yasmin,' the woman suddenly cried. 'There you are!' She ran to the castle and flung her arms around the child.

They hurried away, laughing happily.

Paul and Becky inspected the sad remains of a day's work. They knew it had been worth it.

Thought for the day:

Try to remember what it was like when you were tiny. At times, the world probably seemed a big and scary place.

Something to consider:

Both children and adults have their own view of the world. So it's not surprising if we sometimes have different opinions. Instead of arguing, we should make an effort to understand.

This story was inspired by a girl who lives in India. Her family are desperately poor.

In 2003 many people were dying of heat exhaustion and thirst. They prayed for rain to come. For Radhamma, who suffers from epilepsy, life had become very hard.

Singing in the Rain

Mrs Shivanna stood at the door, glaring angrily at the blue sky. Then she turned and almost in a trance, went back into the house.

Radhamma, lying in a corner of their only room, opened her eyes. She steadied herself against the mud wall and rose to her feet.

'How do you feel?' her mother asked.

'My head aches and I'm thirsty,' said Radhamma. 'I had another fit, didn't I?'

Her mother nodded.

'I'm sure the heat makes me worse,' said Radhamma. 'Why doesn't the monsoon come?'

Mrs Shivanna shrugged her shoulders. 'They say that in Tumkur we're lucky. There's still water in the tap.'

The young girl looked at her anxiously. 'But if it doesn't rain, what then?'

'Have faith. It will come. It must.'

Radhamma bent over the water container and peered inside. 'It's empty again.'

Her mother didn't seem to hear. She sat at the table, her head in her hands.

'I'll go to the tap,' her daughter said. 'I shan't be long.'

She trudged slowly through the village, the earth, baked hard by the sun, scorching the soles of her feet. She looked away as she passed the school. The children were outside, playing in the shade of a tree.

In the distance she could see a line of women waiting for water. As she approached, she heard angry shouting.

'I was here before you.'

'You were not. You pushed in.'

'I didn't. You're a liar.'

Radhamma joined the queue. She watched as a policeman got out of his car. The argument quickly stopped. The woman in front of her turned and smiled wearily.

'Everyone gets impatient in this heat,' she said.

'They've waited two hours to reach the tap.'

Radhamma pulled a face and sat down in the dust. After a while, she started to sing - as she always did. Quietly and sadly. Just to herself.

Suddenly she was aware of a man standing beside her.

It was the policeman. She stopped and glanced up at him.

'Why aren't you in school?' he asked.

'I'm not allowed,' she said. 'They say other children wouldn't understand.'

The policeman looked puzzled. 'Understand what?' he asked.

She couldn't explain. In reply she simply said, 'Epilepsy.'

The policeman shook his head. 'Is that all? But you must go to school. It's your right. I'll talk to your mum and the Headteacher. Just tell me your name - and you'll be in school by next week. I promise!'

He waved to her as he got back in his car.

Radhamma started singing again. But a more cheerful song now. There was hope in her voice.

The next day clouds appeared in the sky. Radhamma walked to the tap as usual - but today everyone seemed to be smiling. When she joined the queue, the woman in front pointed to the sky.

'The monsoon's coming. It's going to rain. Our troubles are over!'

Radhamma felt the first drops of rain on her head. In a matter of moments, it was pouring.

As the rain splashed down, she started to sing. It was the happiest song she had ever sung.

Thought for the day:

Many people suffer from Epilepsy. For some it is no problem. They may simply experience a moment when their mind seems to go blank. But if the Epilepsy is more severe, their arms and legs may start to jerk and, if not sitting, they fall to the ground. Afterwards, they might feel the need to sleep for a short time.

The important thing to remember is not to be frightened. Some of the cleverest people in the world have suffered from it. It hasn't stopped them achieving wonderful things in their lives.

Something to consider:

We take water for granted. Turn on the tap and it's always there. Water is so important to us! In how many ways do we use it? Your list will probably be very long!

When Theresa and Clare entered the BBC Christmas Carol competition they worked so hard - but not in their wildest dreams could they have imagined winning first prize!

A Carol for Shelley

There it was.

The letter inviting Appley School - the tiniest in the country - to go to London to broadcast *their* carol.

The Headteacher held the letter up for everyone to see. They stared at it open-mouthed. It really was true.

At first the two girls were excited. But as the end of term approached, they became more subdued.

'What's the matter with you both?' asked the Headteacher one morning. 'You should be really happy. On Christmas Eve we're going to London!'

'I'm sorry, Mr Blake, I can't go,' said Clare.

'Nor can I,' said Theresa.

He looked shocked. 'What do you mean - can't go?'

'We've always lived in Appley,' said Clare. 'And we've hardly ever gone anywhere. Never to London.'

'Don't worry,' he laughed. 'No one will get lost. I promise!'

'But we can't sing for the BBC. With cameras and lights - and everyone watching. It's too scary.'

'There's no such word as can't,' he said. 'In any case, the whole class are going. Think how disappointed they would be.'

The girls nodded their heads.

'All right,' said Theresa. 'We'll go.'

That evening, Theresa's little sister was bubbling over with excitement.

'I'm coming too, aren't I?' she said.

'No, you can't,' said Theresa. 'You're too young. In any case, you're hopeless at singing.'

'I'm not hopeless - and I am going. Mummy said so.'

'She's not . . . is she?' protested Theresa.

'Yes. Of course,' Mum said. 'I told Mr Blake I would go, to make sure no one gets lost. Shelley can't stay at home alone can she?'

It was Christmas Eve and four o'clock in the morning.

Theresa shone her torch on the path as she hurried along the twisting lanes to the school. Behind her she could just see her mum and Shelley following in the darkness.

'Come on. Hurry up,' she called.

The coach was waiting, engine running and headlights blazing. The Headteacher was standing on the kerb.

'I think you're the last,' he said as he helped them aboard. He walked through the coach, carefully counting. 'We wouldn't want to leave anyone behind, would we? Good, we're all here,' he said. 'We can go.'

Everyone was very quiet as the coach moved off.

'I haven't even had breakfast,' complained Theresa.

'Nor me,' said Clare. 'I couldn't eat anything. I'm too scared.'

It was the longest journey Shelley had ever been on. But just when she thought it would never end, Mr Blake sprang out of his seat.

'We're here,' he said.

Shelley pressed her nose to the window and stared in disbelief. There were such crowds of people on the pavements.

'Where can they all be going?' she thought.

'Now listen carefully,' shouted Mr Blake. 'The Television Centre is enormous. Stay with your group and you won't get lost.'

A smartly dressed lady met them at the door.

'I expect you need to stretch your legs,' she said. 'So before we go to the studio, I'll take you on a tour of the building. Do keep up with me,' she added. 'We haven't a lot of time.'

She smiled, turned and walked briskly down the corridor. It was very confusing. A maze of identical corridors stretched for miles. Doors opened and closed. A continuous stream of people bustled backwards and forwards. They passed men and women clutching important-looking papers, actors muttering to themselves as they rehearsed their lines, and even Father Christmas with a noisy huddle of elves.

'It's time to get ready,' said the smartly dressed lady, glancing at her watch. She led them to a door marked STUDIO FOUR. 'Wait here a moment,' she said.

She listened on her headphone, then opened the door. 'You can go in now,' she said in a hushed voice. 'Someone will tell you where to stand.'

They picked their way round tangled piles of cables, lights, cameras and monitors. People were talking earnestly as they pressed a thousand switches and buttons.

The studio manager beckoned to them. 'Arrange yourselves over here. You sing in ten minutes.'

Mr Blake was feeling nervous. 'I'm sure you'll all sing beautifully,' he said. 'Theresa, don't look so worried. You won't forget your words, will you?'

'No, Mr Blake. That's not the problem,' she whispered. 'It's Shelley. She's not here. We can't sing without her.'

The Headteacher's face turned white. He searched frantically round the room.

There was no sign of her. He whispered urgently to Theresa's mum.

'What's going on?' hissed Clare as she watched them.

Theresa didn't say anything. She just pulled her friend towards the door. Clare looked startled.

'We can't go out now,' she protested.

'We're on television in eight minutes.'

When they were in the corridor Theresa took a deep breath.

'My sister's missing. We've got to find her.'

They hesitated, looking left and right.

Then they ran off into the labyrinth of corridors. Suddenly Clare stopped.

'Look, it's a lift. We came up in it from the News Room.'

Theresa looked doubtful. 'Are you sure? Everywhere looks the same to me.'

'Yes, I'm certain. Don't waste time. Just press the button.'

They stared at the lights above the lift door.

'It's coming down now,' Clare said.

'No. It's stopped. I feel like screaming.'

They glared at the lights, willing the lift to hurry.

'It's started again. Here it comes.'

Theresa glanced anxiously at her watch.

'Only four minutes,' she thought. 'We'll never do it.'

The lift doors opened and a face grinned at them.

'This is great,' laughed Shelley. 'I've never been in a lift before.'

Theresa grabbed her by the arm and they raced back down the corridor.

'We've three minutes,' yelled Theresa.

They ran round the corner, nearly knocking over an elf, and found Mr Blake with their Mum standing at the studio door, looking very agitated.

'Where have you been?' Mum wailed. 'Never mind - tell me later.'

'Get in position quickly,' whispered a voice. 'Sixty seconds to go. Watch my hand for the signal. We're going on air . . . now!'

After they sang the carol, Mr Blake was smiling from ear to ear.

'Well done everyone,' he said. 'That was brilliant.'

'Thanks to Shelley,' said Theresa.

'We were so worried about her, we forgot to be scared!'

Her little sister felt very proud.

Thought for the day:

Caring for each other is more important than anything else!

○ ○ ○ ○ ○ ○ ○ ○ ○

Something to consider:

Do you get worried and anxious about things?

Do you need to stop and remind yourself about what is really important?

Jenny and Jack were desperate to have a pet.
Their dog became more special to them than they could have imagined.

Not Just for Christmas

'Are you *sure* you want a dog?' asked Mrs Brent.

'Of course,' said Jack impatiently.

'Please Mum. We'll *really* look after it,' pleaded Jenny.

'I'm not promising anything. Your Dad will be in soon. See what he says.'

When Mr Brent came through the door, he looked weary. 'Let's stop and think about it,' he said. 'It's not just for Christmas. It's a big commitment. You'd have to take it for walks every day - and pets can be very expensive.'

'Yes. We know that,' said Jack.

'It needn't cost anything Dad,' said Jenny. 'We can get one from the RSPCA.'

'Don't get too excited,' warned Dad the next day. 'Remember - we're only looking. It doesn't mean we're going to have one.'

'You don't have to decide now,' said the RSPCA officer. 'You've seen all the dogs. Phone me tomorrow if you want one.'

'But you didn't show us this one,' Jenny said as they passed a sheep dog poking its nose through the bars. It looked very sad. 'What's its name?'

'Boris,' said the officer.

Immediately, the dog's tail started wagging. His mouth fell open to reveal a long pink tongue and he panted excitedly.

'He's perfect,' gasped Jenny.

'He's certainly friendly enough,' said Mrs Brent. 'What do you think, Jack?'

He crouched down and stared at it.

'Looks good enough to me,' he said.

'He wouldn't really be suitable,' said the officer quickly. 'Boris is blind.'

Jenny stroked the dog's nose gently.

'Poor Boris,' she whispered. 'Come home with us. We'll look after you.'

'Just slow down,' said Dad. 'It's not Christmas yet. You'll have to wait and see. He needs lots of love and care. He's a big responsibility.'

'You're absolutely right, Mr Brent,' said the officer. 'Go home and think about it.'

There was great excitement on Christmas Eve. Boris arrived, and for the next few weeks, the children played with him, raced to feed him, squabbled over brushing him and took him for so many walks, they were quite exhausted. But as the months went by that started to change.

'It's not my turn,' complained Jack one day. 'I took him for a walk yesterday.'

'No you didn't,' said his sister. 'Nor the day before.'

'So what?' said Jack. 'You're the one who really wanted Boris. I didn't.'

Jenny stared at him angrily.

'Well you'll have to look after him on Saturday. I'm going ice skating.'

'But I'm going up to Ten Acre Farm to see Ginger Smith.'

'Too bad,' said Jenny. 'Take Boris with you.'

It was a long, slow walk to the farm, with blind Boris in tow. Jack was relieved when he heard a tractor coming up the lane behind him. It was Ginger's Dad. His son was sitting on the trailer.

'Jump on,' the farmer bellowed.

Boris couldn't stop wagging his tail. He was as pleased as Jack to have a ride. When they came to a halt, Jack let the dog off its lead.

Boris leaped off the trailer and ran round and round the field barking with excitement.

'It's weird,' said Ginger. 'If he can't see, how can he tell where the hedges are? He knows when to turn every time.'

Gradually Boris slowed down. It was a hot day and he was looking tired. They watched as, amazingly, he found his way back to the trailer and lay down in the shade of a wheel.

'Let's go down to the wood. We could do some tree climbing,' suggested Jack.

'But what about the dog?' asked his friend.

'No problem,' said Jack. 'He'll sleep for hours.'

Sure enough, an hour later when they returned, he was still there.

'Told you so,' said Jack.

Nothing appeared to be wrong. They went off to the farmhouse and got a drink. Jack was eating a piece of cake as he wandered back. He could see Boris, still asleep under the trailer.

Farmer Smith had climbed onto the tractor. He waved to them. Then he started the engine. Jack looked at Boris and panicked.

'No!' he screamed at the farmer. 'Don't go!'

The engine roared.

Jack ran like the wind, waving frantically. The wheel of the trailer shuddered.

The dog woke up and raised his head.

Jack dived towards him with outstretched arms. Boris gave a startled yelp. But he was safe, pushed clear of the turning wheel.

Farmer Smith slammed on the brakes - but too late. He found Jack lying on the grass, his face screwed up with pain.

'My arm,' he squealed. 'I think it's broken. The wheel went over it.'

A warm, wet tongue licked his cheek.

Boris wasn't sure what had happened but he knew Jack had done something very special.

Thought for the day:
We must never forget how much animals rely on us.

Something to consider:
Do you have any pets at home?
If so, who takes care of them?

Penny was lonely – before the stranger came along.
'People don't like me because I'm clever,' she used to say.
'They're just jealous.' She didn't have any real friends at all.

Penny's Angel

One year, when it was nearly Christmas, Penny's teacher brought a beautiful tree into school and placed it beside her desk.

'Tomorrow we'll decorate it,' she said. 'I've tinsel and stars and all sorts of things in my cupboard.'

'What happens at the end of term? Will it be thrown away?' Sally Jones asked.

She was a tiny girl, the youngest in the class.

'We'll have a competition,' announced Mrs Cooper. 'The winner can take it home.'

Sally stared at the tree longingly.

'What kind of competition?' she asked.

'The tree needs an angel on top. We'll see who makes the best.'

'That's not fair,' grumbled Barry Clitheroe. 'We all know who'll win - Penny Smith - as usual.'

Mrs Cooper thought very hard.

'I've decided,' she said at last. 'It won't be a competition. Give your angel a name. Write it on a slip of paper and drop it in the pot. It'll be like a raffle. What could be fairer than that?'

It was nearly the end of term. The angels had all been made. They were perched on the bookcase at the back of the room. It was time to find the winner.

Mrs Cooper shook the pot vigorously, plunged in her hand and took out a ticket. Everyone waited expectantly.

'The name is . . . Charity,' she declared.

Immediately, Penny jumped to her feet.

'It's me!' she squealed. 'I knew I'd win!'

'I don't believe it,' snarled Barry.

'I'm sorry,' Mrs Cooper said. 'But it was perfectly fair, wasn't it?'

At the end of the day Penny fixed her angel firmly to the tree. Then she marched out of school carrying it proudly in her arms.

On her way home, she stopped outside Mr Sharrif's corner shop. It was decorated with thousands of tiny lights and a giant inflatable Father Christmas.

'I'm starving. I must buy a chocolate bar,' she thought.

But what could she do with the tree? It was too big to take inside so she leaned it against Father Christmas.

'Look after that for a minute, will you?' she joked.

At that moment little Sally came round the corner. She was wearing a pair of reindeer antlers that flashed red and green.

Penny poked out her tongue. Then she lunged at Sally, grabbed the antlers and ran across the road.

She waved them in the air.

'Catch me if you can,' she yelled.

Sally paused briefly, then chased after her. She didn't look left or right.

A car, travelling much too fast, slammed on its brakes and screeched to a halt.

'You'll get yourself killed!' shouted the driver.

Sally's face had turned white. Still trembling, she hurried after Penny who was now skipping down the road.

Suddenly Penny stretched up and hooked the antlers onto a road sign.

'Have the stupid things - if you can reach them!' she taunted. She wandered off, laughing.

Of course, Sally was far too short. She jumped and jumped but no matter how hard she tried it was impossible. Close to tears, she stood on the pavement, wondering what to do.

'All right, wimp,' said Penny.

She came slowly back, snatched the antlers down and tossed them to her.

'There. Now say thank you,' she sneered.

It was then that she noticed a Christmas tree displayed in a shop window.

'The tree!' she thought. 'How could I forget it!'

Ignoring Sally, she raced back across the road. When she reached the shop she glared at Father Christmas.

'It's gone. Someone's pinched it,' she muttered angrily.

She rushed inside. Mr Sharrif leaned on the counter and beamed at her.

'What can I do for you, young lady?' he asked.

'Someone stole a Christmas tree from outside your shop. I left it there ten minutes ago.'

'Stole? No, I don't think so,' chuckled Mr Sharrif. 'A woman came in just now with a small child. They looked very poor. 'I want to buy a tree', she said. 'We've sold out,' I said. She said I hadn't. She had seen one outside.

I was surprised. The last one was sold hours ago. I was sure. So I said, 'If there's one left over, you're welcome to it. Free. No charge. Spread a bit of happiness. You get twice as much back. That's what I say.'

'I just want my tree back,' cried Penny as she ran to the door. 'Or, at least, I think I do.'

'If you're quick, you'll catch her,' said Mr Sharrif. 'She can't have gone far.'

Penny stepped outside and looked up and down the street.

'That's odd,' she gasped.

There was no sign of anyone. But instead, there was Charity - Penny's angel - lying at her feet.

She picked it up and glanced at it. As she did so, she imagined a day long, long ago in Bethlehem. And she thought of the poor woman and her child - at home today with the beautiful tree.

'My gift,' Penny thought. 'Spread a bit of happiness. That's what I say!'

Thought for the day:

Giving can bring as much happiness as receiving. Perhaps this is what Christmas is all about.

Something to consider:

It's easy to write a letter to Father Christmas with a list of what we want. He would be surprised if you wrote asking for gifts for someone else. Why not try?

Beth never seemed to think of other people - until, one Christmas, she had a nasty shock!

The Silver Pig

Beth came downstairs clutching a bulging stocking. 'Happy Christmas,' she called.

'Happy Christmas,' said Mum. 'Anything exciting in there?'

'Yes, fantastic. Thanks Mum.'

Brian, her little brother, was fizzing with excitement. He rushed up to her, quite out of breath.

'Father Christmas has been! Just look at this,' he said, holding up a sock full of presents. 'You'll never guess what's in here.'

'You're right. I'll never guess - so tell me,' his sister said.

'Colouring pens, a funny false nose, a green sugar mouse, loads of sweets, a chocolate orange and right at the bottom - my favourite - an 'Ear-Blaster' electric horn for my bike!'

Beth wasn't interested. She had crept to the door of the front room and was peering in.

A mountain of presents was piled under the tree. An Aladdin's cave!

'Can we open them now?' she called.

'After Christmas dinner,' a voice answered from the kitchen. 'Make yourself useful, will you? Come and help with the vegetables.'

Beth groaned impatiently. 'Shan't be a minute,' and she wandered over to the tree and gazed down at the gifts.

'I wonder . . . how many are mine?' She got down on her hands and knees and started counting.

'Not bad,' she muttered. 'More than last year - and some big ones too.'

'Where are you Beth?' called her Mum. 'Granddad will be here soon and the potatoes still need peeling.'

'Shan't be long, Mum. I'm just tidying up.'

One by one she put the gifts back under the tree, counting again as she did so.

'I'm right,' she said happily. 'Thirteen! And Brian's only got ten!' She stood up and sniffed the air.

'Roast turkey. Delicious,' Beth thought. She went towards the kitchen, then changed her mind. Instead she wandered into the dining room.

The table was laid for four, with the best plates and dishes - and some beautiful crackers.

'I bet they're from Burlington's in the High Street,' she muttered. 'They must have cost a fortune!'

She picked up each in turn, shook it, held it above her head and squinted inside. There was nothing interesting in three of them. But the fourth was different. It was difficult to be sure but it looked like a lucky charm. A tiny silver pig.

'That's the one for me,' she whispered.

She studied the table for a moment. 'Mum will sit . . . there,' she thought. 'Brian sits . . . there. Granddad . . . there.' She tapped her finger on the table. 'And I shall sit here – so that must be my cracker.'

'Where are you Beth? I need you.'

It was Mum calling again.

'Just coming,' Beth answered and hurried to the kitchen.

'You're too late. I've done the vegetables now. Granddad's at the door. Go and let him in.'

An hour later Granddad glared at the lonely sprout on his plate.

'It's beaten me,' he said. 'That was the best meal I can remember.'

'Anyone for trifle?' asked Mum.

'Me – please,' said Brian.

'And me!' said Beth. Then she hesitated. 'We haven't pulled the crackers yet. Let's do it now!'

She rattled hers, held it up and peered inside. Yes - definitely the silver pig.

'Help me pull it, Brian,' she demanded.

'Just a minute,' said Mum. 'Let me finish serving the trifle.'

But Beth couldn't wait. She stretched across the table, waving the cracker at her brother.

'Hold tight and pull,' she demanded.

Brian did as he was told. He pulled and pulled.

'Crack!'

The cracker suddenly burst open.

'Here's your party hat - under my chair,' laughed Mum.

'And here's a joke,' said Granddad, rescuing a slip of paper from the custard.

'What happens to a flea when it becomes angry?'

'I know,' said Brian. 'It gets hopping mad!'

Beth didn't think it at all funny.

'It's somewhere on the table!' she snarled as she searched among the dishes.

'What is?' asked Mum. 'A flea?'

'No,' snapped Beth irritably. 'Something that was in the cracker.'

'It can't be far away. Look for it later - after you've eaten your trifle.' Brian had almost finished his. He'd gobbled it in a flash.

'I'm full to bursting,' he gasped. 'I swallowed a hard bit just now. What was that?'

'Just a nut, I expect,' said Mum.

Opening the presents should have been fun. And so it was - for Beth. But her brother didn't look happy. He had turned very pale.

Mum started to feel worried.

'Brian, are you all right?' she asked.

'Tummy ache,' he groaned. 'Don't feel well.'

'Go and lie down. You'll feel as right as rain by teatime.'

But instead, as the evening wore on, he felt worse. Tears trickled down his face.

'It hurts a lot,' he cried.

Mum tried to reassure him.

'It's just something you've eaten,' she said.

Beth started to panic. 'The silver pig,' she thought.

She rushed back to the dining room and searched frantically.

Mum appeared at the door.

'Why are you so upset? It was only something silly from a cracker! I'm worried about your brother,' she added. 'If he isn't much better by the morning, we'll have to get the doctor.'

Beth tossed and turned in bed that night. She hardly slept at all. And when she did, she had a terrible nightmare.

'The pig fell in the trifle,' she whispered. 'Brian's ill and it's my fault.'

Late the next morning, Mum poked her head round the bedroom door.

'Are you getting up?' she asked. 'I thought you'd like to know, your brother's as fit as a fiddle this morning - it was just indigestion. By the way, is this what you were looking for? A silver pig! I found it under the table. Perhaps it'll bring you luck!'

Thought for the day:
Christmas presents are exciting but how quickly do you get bored with them?

Something to consider:
What memories do you have of last Christmas? Was it just the presents that made it special?

The boy in this story thought that it was his lucky day. But things don't always turn out the way we expect!

Lost and Found

Andy was half way through the garden gate when he saw it. A crumpled £20 note on the edge of the pavement. He stooped to pick it up.

'It can't be real,' he thought.

But it was!

Someone must have dropped it. He glanced round uneasily. Perhaps it was a trick. Was someone hiding - waiting to see what he would do?

No. The street was deserted.

'It's not stealing,' he reassured himself. 'If I don't have it, someone else will.'

He quickly stuffed it in his coat pocket and hurried to the house.

Andy was humming happily when he walked through the door.

'You must have had a good day. You're like a dog with two tails,' said Mum. 'Get that old coat off and wash your hands. Tea's ready.'

He ran up the stairs, flung his coat on the bed - hesitated - and picked it up again. Suddenly he was uneasy. Suppose Mum found the money. How could he explain it? What would he say?

'I need to hide it,' he thought. 'Somewhere safe. Somewhere really safe,' he repeated slowly.

But he had to feast his eyes on his £20 just one more time before going down to tea. 'What are you doing Andy?' called his mum. 'Your tea's getting cold.'

He stuffed his fortune back into the pocket of his coat, which he then hastily pushed under his bed.

'That's as good as anywhere, at least for the moment,' he thought.

At school the next day, it was difficult for Andy to concentrate.

'Should I have told Mum?' he wondered.

The question nagged at him.

'No! The money's mine. Why should I feel guilty? I'm not a thief.'

By the time he got home again, he had a long shopping list in his mind.

'That's the problem,' he thought. 'There's so much I want. £20 isn't enough. I wish it was more.'

His mum was in the kitchen.

'I've a nice surprise for you,' she said. 'I won some money on the Lotto yesterday. Tomorrow's Saturday so we'll go to the shops and buy you a new coat.'

'Thanks Mum, but I don't need one. My old one's fine.'

'It's no good arguing,' Mum said. 'I found your old one upstairs today and took it to Oxfam. Someone will be pleased.'

Andy swallowed hard.

'But Mum,' he protested. 'You can't give it away. I need it. I've got to have it.'

Mum shrugged her shoulders.

'Too late now. It's gone.'

The next morning Mum was looking worried.

'I've lost my prize money. It was £20. I've searched everywhere. Even outside on the pavement.'

Andy's face turned white. He dashed from the room.

'I'm going out for a while,' he called. 'I shan't be long.'

The door slammed and he ran like the wind.

When he reached the shops he was gasping for breath. Oxfam was already busy. It was crowded with customers - many trying on coats. The weather had suddenly turned cold.

Andy searched desperately.

'They can't have sold it yet. My coat must be here,' he muttered. 'It's just got to be.'

But it wasn't.

Someone had an early and unexpected Christmas present. They must have been very pleased!

Thought for the day:
Sometimes we are faced with difficult decisions. But if we don't know what to do, our conscience will tell us.

Something to consider:
Do you think the money Andy found was his mother's?
Even if it wasn't, should he have kept it? What would you have done?

What would Lucy's New Year's Resolution be?

Too Valuable to Lose

It was the last day of the Christmas holiday and she still hadn't decided.

'Lucy, you're not doing anything. Go down to Supersave, will you?' said her mum. 'There are a few things we need.'

Lucy looked out of the window. The sky was grey and there was a flurry of snow in the air.

She pulled up her coat collar as she wandered down the road.

'Shopping!' she thought. 'What a boring way to end the holiday. I wish something exciting would happen.'

It was then that she noticed something lying in the gutter. She picked it up. It was a ring mounted with three beautiful red stones.

'It must be valuable,' she thought as she tried it on her finger.

'A pity - it's much too big. I must be careful I don't lose it.'

By the time she came to pay for her shopping it had slipped off so many times, she was glad to drop it in her bag.

'It'll be safe there,' she muttered.

As she walked out of the store, she noticed her friend Amy. She ran up to her.

'Amy, what are you doing here?' she asked.

They looked at each other's heavy bags.

'Stupid question!' Amy said. 'Let's walk along together. Mum needs this shopping and I've got to get my stuff together for school.'

'Wait a minute. Just see what I've found,' said Lucy. 'An incredible ring. It's here, in the bottom of my bag.'

But Amy wasn't interested.

'Snow!' she gasped. 'We were only in the shop a short time - and now look at it!'

The air was filled with drifting flakes and the road was covered with a layer that crunched under their feet as they walked.

It was strangely quiet.

Only half an hour before, the town had been so busy. Now, it was almost deserted. The two girls screwed up their eyes and made for home as quickly as they could, their coats firmly buttoned against the icy wind.

As soon as they reached Lucy's house they flung the bags down.

'We could make a snowman,' Lucy said. 'The biggest in the world!'

'Come on then. Let's get started,' laughed her friend.

Lucy watched her for a moment.

'My New Year's Resolution,' she thought. 'Friends are valuable - so I must be nice to them.'

The snowman took a long time to finish. It was far taller than the girls. They were standing admiring it when the door opened and Lucy's mum appeared.

'There you are, Lucy. I was getting worried. Can you bring the shopping in quickly?'

'It must be late,' said Amy. 'I'll be in trouble. See you tomorrow.'

She grabbed a bag and rushed off down the road.

Lucy waved and went quickly into the house. Her mum was angry.

'You silly girl,' she shouted. 'What did you buy all this for? I gave you a list. Why didn't you read it?'

Lucy stared at the shopping.

'I don't understand. Those aren't the things I bought,' she said.

Then she guessed what had happened.

'Amy was in such a hurry. She went off with our shopping.'

Suddenly there was a knock on the door.

'That'll be her now,' she thought.

She sighed with relief when she opened the door and found her friend waiting.

'Here's your bag,' Amy said breathlessly. 'I slipped on the pavement and dropped it, so I hope nothing's broken.'

As Lucy returned to the kitchen she remembered the ring. She unpacked the shopping as fast as she could.

'Just see what I've got,' she said. 'I found it on the road. It must be worth a fortune.'

Lucy stared into the bag. She turned it inside out.

'I don't believe it. She's stolen it! No one else knew it was there . . . Just you wait Amy Brown. I'll get you for this!'

'There won't be any school today,' Lucy said to her mum the next morning. 'The bus won't be able to get through. The snow's really deep.'

'It's not as bad as it looks,' her mum replied. 'It should be on time so you'd better hurry.'

Sure enough, as Lucy ran to the bus stop, it appeared at the end of the road. She climbed on, smouldering with anger. Amy was sitting at the back. She walked towards her, glaring furiously. Amy smiled and gave a little wave. Lucy let out a cry of rage and ran at her. There, on her friend's finger, was a ring. Her ring. She recognised it immediately. She grabbed her by the hair and pulled.

'You're a thieving toad. I hate you. I'll never speak to you again,' she screamed.

'Stop it. Get off me,' her friend pleaded. 'What have I done to you?'

'Don't act so innocent,' snarled Lucy. The ring. My ring. You stole it.'

'I didn't,' protested Amy. 'It was in my Christmas stocking.'

At that moment the bus driver caught Lucy by the arm.

'No fighting on my bus,' he snapped. 'Get off now. You can walk.'

Lucy stood crying beside the road. She watched the bus disappear in the distance. Then she walked home.

'I don't feel well,' she said to her mum. 'I'm going to bed.'

Late that afternoon, her dad knocked on her bedroom door.

'How are you?' he asked.

'I've brought something to cheer you up. Look at this.'

He held up a ring. It was mounted with three beautiful red stones.

Lucy felt confused.

'How did you get it?' she asked.

'I've been clearing the snow,' he said. 'I found it lying on our path. Someone must have dropped it.'

Lucy took it from him and gazed at it thoughtfully.

'Don't get too excited,' he said. 'It isn't worth anything. The toy shop has a window full of them.'

Thought for the day:

What's more valuable - the things we own - or our friends?

Something to consider:

Have you made a New Year's Resolution?

How soon do you think you'll forget it?

If you've ever visited a lifeboat station, you'll have seen a powerful rescue vessel, with all the latest equipment, ready to be launched at a moment's notice, in even the fiercest storm.

This story is about events that took place 150 years ago when things were very different.

Impossible

Anne was lonely. Visitors rarely appeared in her village. The journey by horse and cart following rocky tracks across high, windswept hills was long and difficult.

To get there by sea was no easier. The tiny harbour was overshadowed by sheer granite cliffs where ships could be dashed to pieces on the rocks.

Often Anne would sit in her father's huge rowing boat on the quayside. She would imagine him with the other men, straining on the oars, battling to rescue survivors from the angry sea.

One cold February morning she stood with a crowd of villagers, huddled against a biting north wind, on the jetty. They were waiting for a new ship to pass, on its maiden voyage to India. Sam Vellacott, the publican of the King's Head, was sure it would leave from Bristol that day.

'It'll be a grand sight,' he said. 'The prettiest sailing ship you'll ever see.'

But by midday the wind was whipping the waves into such a frenzy that even the church tower was hard to see through the spray.

Anne shuddered and clutched her shawl more tightly around her.

'We might as well go home,' said Sam to Anne's father. 'No captain would risk bringing his ship close to shore in weather like this.'

Anne felt disappointed.

The crowd gradually dispersed to the warmth of their homes. Soon only Anne and her father remained, staring anxiously into the stinging rain. Heavy storm clouds swept across the sky and it quickly became dark.

'You'd think it was night,' yelled her father. 'Even if she's out there we shan't see her. There's no point in staying longer.'

Anne nodded. Her hands were frozen.

Suddenly, as she clung to her father's arm, the rain eased and the sky lightened.

Anne gasped with horror.

She could see a huge ship drifting into the bay. It was still some way off but clearly it was in terrible danger.

Two masts were broken and its sails torn to shreds.

'Sound the alarm!'

Although her Dad's voice was carried away in the wind Anne knew what had to be done.

She waited as a wave broke over the jetty, then ran to the warning bell. A tightly lashed rope prevented it moving in the wind. For some minutes she wrestled with the knot. At last it came free and she pulled.

The huge bell started to swing backwards and forwards, backwards and forwards. Its slow, mournful sound rang out again and again. As it echoed through the village, men were racing through the narrow streets to the harbour. By the time Anne got there, some were already in the boat, yelling orders to the others as they heaved it slowly to the slipway.

Then she ran to her father. He was standing a little way off, his eyes screwed up against the storm.

'Dad! Aren't you going? They're waiting for you.'

'It's not me they're waiting for. We can't launch in a north wind,' he shouted.

A figure appeared, calling out through the driving rain.

'We're ready. Now just pray for the wind to ease.'

Anne stood with her mother, taking one last look at the deserted boat still poised above the slipway. Her father and the other men had waited patiently. At last they'd all retreated to the King's Arms.

'Come on. We'd better go home and get dry,'

Anne looked pleadingly at her mum.

'There must be something we can do. People are going to die.'

Her mum shook her head.

'They can't launch in a north wind.'

'There's got to be a way,' gasped Anne. She paused, staring out to sea. Now and again the stricken ship appeared through the waves.

'The east side of the headland! Why not launch from there? They could, couldn't they?'

'No,' said a voice behind her. She glanced round. Her dad was there. 'No one could drag a boat over Hangman Hill. It's too steep. It's impossible. You know it is.'

Anne glared at him.

'How can you say that? At least we could try.'

We'll never know how Anne convinced her dad - or how he convinced everyone else in the village.

'It's madness,' said Sam as he sat drinking his beer in the King's Head. 'But my old mum always said I was a bit daft. Come on. Let's have a go.'

Amazingly, within a short space of time, ropes were found and lines of men and women were soon hauling the boat up the hill. Anne and her friends threw stones under the slipping wheels and other children ran to and fro with drinks and food.

The people were close to despair. The boat was so heavy and the hill so steep. By the time they reached the top, no one had the energy to cheer.

The slope was even steeper on the east side. It was slow, backbreaking work, sliding in the deep mud as they held back their heavy load.

The storm was still raging when at last the lifeboat entered the churning water.

'Ready?' yelled Anne's dad. He looked at the other men. 'Heave!'

Oars dipped into the waves. Slowly the boat disappeared into the night.

'A hundred years from now, people will read about this day,' said Anne's granddad as he watched. 'They won't believe it.'

She looked at him anxiously.

'Don't worry,' he said. 'Your dad's a good sailor. He'll come home safe.'

Although Anne was exhausted she couldn't sleep that night. It was still early when she ran down to the harbour. Half the village were already there, gazing out to sea. The wind had dropped and it was calm. In the distance, seagulls were circling above some drifting planks.

There was nothing else.

Anne felt ill with grief. She burst into tears and ran blindly away. It didn't matter where. Nothing mattered any more.

Without thinking, she climbed and climbed until she found herself on the high ridge of Barrow Point. The small beach below was in shadow.

Beyond it, through her tears, she could see wreckage floating wherever she looked. Suddenly she heard a sound. Someone was below her on the still dark beach. It hardly seemed possible. Surely that was the shape of a boat lying at a crazy angle among the rocks?

Anne scrambled towards it, hardly daring to hope. There were shapes huddled beside it. Not moving.

Then, as her mother, granddad, and half the village plunged down the slope behind her, she saw an arm weakly waving. Her dad and his crew were alive.

It seemed a miracle. Lying close by were the ship's captain and his two young daughters. Safe. Plucked from the sea as the ship was dashed to pieces against the cliffs. They were carried to the King's Arms, to be looked after by Sam Vellacott and his wife.

A tiny cottage near the harbour had stood empty for a long time. When they had recovered from their ordeal, the captain and his daughters went to look at it. They decided to make it their home.

Anne never felt lonely again.

Thought for the day:

Never be too quick to say something is impossible. Throughout history people have done amazing things.

Something to consider:

Was Anne right to encourage her father and his friends to risk their lives?

Many years ago, a scientist dared to say that the earth isn't flat – and that our world revolves around the sun! His name was Galileo. He was imprisoned and threatened with death - simply for saying what he knew to be true!

He could have complained that life isn't fair.

Exactly 300 years after he died, another great scientist was born.
He too might have complained, 'It's not fair.' But he didn't.

Making the Most of It

Stephen was born in London.

The Second World War was raging fiercely - it was a frightening and dangerous time. Bombs were dropping, night after night; the air was filled with explosions, sirens and shouting.

One Saturday evening Stephen's parents had taken him with them to visit some friends.

'It's getting late,' said his dad, glancing at his watch. 'We'd better get home while it's still quiet.'

He had hardly finished speaking when, in the distance, he heard the muffled sound of bombs.

'They've started early. Come on Stephen, let's get your coat on quickly. It'll be cold outside.'

His mother put him in his pushchair. Then, after a hasty goodbye, they gathered up their gas masks and hurried into the night.

As they ran through the streets, Stephen stared up at the dark houses silhouetted against a red sky. Every few moments there were blinding flashes and ground-shaking crashes.

'A bad storm tonight,' Dad shouted to his son. 'Nothing to worry about.'

Stephen felt reassured and smiled happily as they rushed on.

'We're nearly home,' yelled Mum.

Her voice was drowned by an ear splitting noise, a fiery blast of wind - and all Stephen could see was smoke and dust.

'How did that happen?' he wondered when the air started to clear. His mum and dad were sprawled on top of him in a doorway.

They staggered to their feet and dragged Stephen's pushchair through the rubble.

'Look,' screamed Mum. 'Our house has gone!'

Dad stared into the chaos of flaming ruins. He gasped with relief.

'No,' he said. 'It's the house next door.'

The war came to an end - but Stephen's troubles weren't over. Children at school teased and bullied him. He was a small, skinny boy. His uniform was always a mess and he talked so quickly, he was difficult to understand.

His house was cluttered with books, the carpets were threadbare and the furniture shabby.

Unfinished homework, pots of glue, books, bits of model aircraft and mugs of half-drunk tea were scattered around his room.

'I bet you a bag of sweets,' said one child to another at school. 'Stephen will never succeed at anything.'

He could so easily have been right.

Stephen spent most of his days thinking. He was fascinated by everything - life, the world, the stars and the universe.

'Why? How? What's it all about?' he thought.

He wanted to know.

'I'll work hard - and become a scientist,' he decided.

But it wasn't to be easy!

Stephen became very ill. As the years went by he grew thinner and thinner and was soon completely paralysed.

But he was determined to work on, even from his wheelchair.

'I try to make the most of every moment,' he said. 'Life isn't fair. You just have to do the best you can.'

Against all the odds, Stephen Hawking was to become one of the greatest scientists the world has ever known.

Another Galileo!

Thought for the day:

People are often faced with enormous difficulties in their lives but through courage and determination have achieved great things.

Something to consider:

Have you ever found something so difficult, you were tempted to give up? What happened?

In the year 1642 there was a bitter argument between the English king, Charles 1st, and his parliament. It was the start of a terrible war.

What should people do? Support the Royalists and fight for their king?
Or join Parliament's army – the Roundheads?
It was a difficult choice.

The Gardener's Daughter

A young girl in a faded blue dress watched royal flags fluttering on the castle walls.

'Look. There's my dad,' Lizzy said proudly as a man waved down to her.

'What's he doing up there?' laughed her friend, a small, sandy haired boy. 'He must be crazy. Hundreds of Roundheads might arrive at any minute. What can a gardener do? Throw cabbages at them?'

Lizzy looked indignant. 'He'll fight if he has to. Lady Bankes and her girls are almost alone in the castle. There's hardly anyone to protect them.'

'Against five hundred Roundheads? They won't stand a chance!'

Suddenly, Joseph the blacksmith, red-faced and flustered, ran past.

'What you kids doing? Don't just stand there!' he shouted. 'Get away while you can.'

The boy didn't hesitate. He left Lizzy's side and rushed off.

Lizzy, too frightened to move, could only stand and watch the soldiers marching straight towards her. Dressed in leather and steel, she knew immediately who they were!

'Halt!' bellowed a voice.

A giant of a man with a drooping, black moustache strode forward, clutching a sheet of paper. He smiled at Lizzy.

She glared.

'We're your friends,' he beamed. 'You'll run a little errand for us, won't you?'

Lizzy tried hard to look fierce. He bent closer; she could smell his breath. She drew back, clenched her fists and stuck out her chin defiantly.

He gave her the paper.

'It's important. Just deliver it, will you? There's a good girl.' He smiled but his eyes were cold as ice.

Lizzy nodded.

As she crossed the bridge and approached the main gate, heads appeared over the ramparts.

'Lizzy Bower, what are you doing here?'

'It's a message from the Roundheads.' She waved the paper in the air.

For a long time nothing happened. Lizzy looked up at the portcullis and the enormous door of oak and iron and waited. Then, clanking and creaking, the portcullis slowly rose.

'Far enough!' bellowed a voice.

Lizzy crawled under. At the same time the door behind it opened, sufficiently for her to squeeze through.

It slammed behind her.

'Follow me,' ordered a guard.

They ran across the deserted outer bailey and reached the inner ward. Then they plunged into a labyrinth of narrow, winding corridors and stairs. The view from a window told her that they were now high in the castle keep. Eventually the guard stopped and knocked at a small, heavy door. He pushed it open.

'The Governor,' he said.

A tired-looking man rose slowly from his desk.

'You have something for me,' he said quietly.

Lizzy felt out of breath. She didn't say anything as she handed him the paper.

He studied it, then flung it on the floor. He looked at Lizzy for a moment. Then he laughed.

'Only two of my men killed and they expect me to surrender? They're fools! Tell them that!'

The guard beckoned to her. She followed him out of the room, but although she tried to keep up, he was running so fast that she dropped further and further behind. The silent corridors were dark and confusing.

Suddenly she stopped. There was no sign of him. Which way had he gone? There were doors to left and right. One was slightly open and, after a moment's hesitation, she pushed it. She found herself in an elegant room. The walls were hung with rich tapestries and the ceiling decorated with ornate plaster designs. So different to the little smoke-filled parlour of her cottage in the village!

Six girls were huddled together beside the biggest fireplace she had ever seen. She recognised them at once. The daughters of Lady Bankes.

She felt bewildered. What should she do?

One of them looked at her.

'It's little Lizzy from the village! How did you get here? A messenger from the outside world! No one tells us anything. Is the war over yet?'

Lizzy shook her head. 'The castle's surrounded.'

'Again?' gasped one of the girls. 'This can't go on. What can we do?'

'Surrender,' said Sarah, the youngest sister. 'It's hopeless. We've cannon and muskets - and no one to use them!'

They all stared miserably into the fireplace. Lizzy took a deep breath.

'Why don't we fire them?' she said. 'We could - with some help.'

There was silence.

'Why not?' Lizzy pleaded desperately.

'All right. Better than sitting here,' said Sarah suddenly. 'Let's give them a nasty shock!'

She ran to the door. The twins, Tess and Charlotte, looked at each other.

'Come on,' said Tess. 'If we don't look after them, they'll get their heads blown off.'

A large picnic table had been set up beside the church. Colonel Bingham happily ate a leg of chicken as he watched his Roundhead troop ripping lead off the church roof. It would make excellent bullets.

Suddenly there was an explosion and a cannonball roared past him. It glanced off the wall and pieces of stone flew everywhere.

The colonel fell off his chair. Seconds later another ball hurtled past. It almost hit a Roundhead who was quietly cleaning his musket.

Shot after shot rang out from the castle. Cannonballs were flying in all directions.

'Keep your heads down!' shouted the colonel as he sprawled on the ground.

In that first hour, everyone - including Lady Bankes and the girls - raced frantically from gun to gun. When they eventually stopped for a rest Colonel Bingham breathed a sigh of relief.

History tells us that the final siege lasted thirteen weeks! But in February 1646 a traitor opened the gates. Disguised as Royalists, the enemy were through the outer bailey and into the inner ward before anyone knew what had happened. The castle was captured at last.

Colonel Bingham was waiting impatiently outside. He strode up and down.

'I've waited long enough. Bring out the prisoners now,' he demanded.

To his amazement, Lizzy's dad, the gardener, marched through the gate. He was beating a drum. With him were seven young girls. One was Lizzy, holding high the royal banner.

Lady Bankes and fifteen men walked behind.

Five hundred Roundheads watched and wondered. Colonel Bingham felt confused.

'This was our enemy?' he thought.

Suddenly he took off his hat.

He threw it in the air and shouted 'Well done!'

Immediately, everyone was cheering.

'Well done,' they echoed. 'Well done.'

Thought for the day:
People are capable of great acts of courage, even in the face of disaster.

Something to consider:
Corfe Castle was one of the most powerful fortresses in England. Perhaps you can find out more about it – and other castles too.

Henry wasn't the bravest of creatures but one day he had to face his fears.

Big Feet

'Henry, you're a coward. You're frightened of everything,' said his mum. 'Just look at your brothers and sisters. They learned how to swim without even thinking about it. Whoever heard of a duck that was frightened of water? And what's your problem with flying?' she demanded.

'My feet are too big. They get in the way. In any case, I can't stand heights,' said Henry. 'I get dizzy.'

'If you've never flown, how can you possibly know?'

Henry didn't say anything. He waddled off beside the river, deep in thought. Suddenly he tripped, slid down the bank and splashed into the water. A group of passing moorhens sniggered and jeered.

Henry ignored them. He pecked at some passing weed. Then, pretending he hadn't a care in the world, he closed his eyes and let the current carry him swiftly down stream.

'Look where you're going!' shouted a voice. 'Remember the rule of the river.'

Henry opened his eyes again and hastily back paddled. He had almost collided with a magnificent swan.

'Rule of the river? What rule?'

'Look after each other. That rule! The river's a dangerous place.'

Henry nodded. He struggled to turn around, but controlling his feet was difficult. They really were unusually large.

The swan preferred not to watch. She shook her head despairingly and hid her head under her wing.

In fact, Henry only spun around twice before heading in the right direction. The moorhens were settling down for the night under the old boathouse when he passed. This time they didn't laugh. He was travelling at an impressive speed.

The sun was setting by the time he reached home. Some ducks flew over. He listened to the flap of their wings and sighed.

'I'm sure I could fly . . . if only my feet weren't so big.'

Next day the swan was admiring herself in the water by the boathouse when she heard barking.

Suddenly, to her horror, an enormous wolfhound burst through the bushes where Henry was dozing in the sun. The frightened swan snorted and hissed loudly.

Henry woke up startled and found the snarling hound towering over him. Its open jaws revealed razor sharp teeth. Its hot breath made poor Henry blink. He leaped to his feet, turned and ran for his life.

Snap! The jaws had closed.

Henry lost a tail feather but didn't look back. His big flat feet pounded the ground. He gained speed. He beat his wings, faster and faster.

The dog sprang at him.

One desperate quack. One final thump of feet and flap of wings. Henry was in the air, flying!

It's hard to say who was more surprised - Henry, now perched dizzily on the boathouse roof, or the angry hound below.

'How did I do that?' thought Henry.

The swan, chuckling quietly to herself, drifted closer.

The hound snarled. He clawed the ground.

There was a bloodcurdling bark. The next moment he was in the water, swimming furiously towards her.

The swan backed away.

'Remember the rule!' Henry thought. He hardly dared to look down. Did he jump or did he fall? It all happened so quickly.

As his heavy feet struck the hound's back, even animals far away heard that final, fearful bark.

Then there was silence.

Moorhens came out cautiously from the reeds.

'Henry saved my life - and drowned,' said the swan sadly.

'He pretended he couldn't fly,' said an amazed moorhen.

'He was so modest,' said another.

'And brave,' laughed a familiar voice.

Everyone cheered with excitement as Henry scrambled out of the water and stood dripping on the bank. He took a deep breath, waddled as fast as he could, spread his wings and took a gigantic leap.

'I'm flying,' he cried happily as with feet tucked under his tail he rose gracefully into the evening sky.

Thought for the day:
It's easy to think up excuses to avoid things we fear.

Something to consider:
Are there things you are too frightened to try?

This is the story of Helen, a girl who showed great courage in her life.

Why Not?

Mrs Draycott sighed as she looked at the clock.

'The match should have finished ages ago,' she said crossly.

Her husband stared at his cold cup of tea.

'Helen really enjoys football - and she's good at it. She's one of the best,' he said. 'That doesn't stop me worrying,' said Mrs Draycott. 'We've told her before. Unless she comes straight home - she can't play in the team.'

'I'm in trouble,' thought Helen. 'But it's not my fault. The game didn't even start on time.'

To make matters worse, when she left the school gate, she noticed fog descending. It hadn't seemed so bad in the street lights. Now, as she turned into Woodlands Lane, it was becoming frighteningly thick.

'Keep calm,' she told herself. 'Just follow the path.'

But as she stared at the hedgerow her heart beat faster. Was that a movement? A rustling of leaves?

She stood still. What should she do? The next moment a small animal scurried across the path. Helen gasped with relief.

'I'm being stupid,' she said to herself. 'I walk home this way every day from school. It's safe enough.'

Then she froze. There was definitely someone there, slowly emerging through the fog.

'Where am I? Can you help me?' wailed a timid voice. Out of nowhere an old lady appeared.

'I'm hopelessly lost. How do I get to Canal Cottage?'

'That's no problem,' said Helen. 'It's not far from here. I'll come with you.'

She clutched the old lady's arm, turned round and steered her back down the lane. As they approached the canal, the fog became dense.

Helen groped blindly forwards. Suddenly she bumped into some railings. She recognised them.

'I know where we are,' she said. 'Look, it's a gravel path. Your cottage is really close.'

'So it is,' chuckled the old lady. 'Thank you. You're very kind.'

Of course, as Helen suspected, when she arrived home she was in trouble! She was very late. Mum and Dad were furious.

'No excuses!' shouted Mum. 'We've been worried sick about you.'

'You're going nowhere for a week,' growled Dad.

'Not even for football?' gasped Helen.

'Definitely not,' snapped Dad.

She felt like crying. It really wasn't her fault, was it?

It was twenty years later.

A house was burning fiercely. Helen glanced down at the steadily growing crowd. An ambulance had arrived with siren wailing and blue lights flashing.

She clung on as the ladder was manoeuvred towards the building. Black smoke was belching from an open window. She calculated the distance. Just one metre more. She leaned forward. Then she jumped and disappeared into the smoke. Below, the crowd gasped. The window below was spitting monstrous plumes of flame.

'She'll never get out alive,' said a policeman.

Then someone pointed excitedly.

'Look. Up there!'

Two figures were balanced on a narrow ledge. There was a hushed silence. Helen grabbed the top of the ladder and leaped onto it, pulling a terrified old lady with her. Not a moment too soon.

Glass started shattering in the heat and as the ladder swung away, there was a noise like thunder.

Walls were tumbling. A choking cloud of dust filled the air. What was happening? No one could see.

But as the dust drifted away the crowd gasped. Two people were lying together in the road. They were very still. Then a hand moved - and an arm.

Slowly, painfully, the fire fighter and the old lady pulled themselves to their feet. Helen wiped the soot from her eyes and smiled. She remembered another old lady, many years before.

The next moment the crowd were rushing towards them, cheering so loudly they could be heard on the far side of town.

'I'll be a fire fighter when I grow up,' said a boy.

'So shall I,' said his little sister.

'You can't be,' the boy said. 'You're only a girl.'

A policeman looked down at her.

'Why not?' he said. 'You could be like Helen. She's one of the best.'

Thought for the day:

With determination, anything in life may be possible.

What's your opinion?

Helen was late and knew her parents would be worried. Do you think she was right to help the old lady in the fog?

This is the true story about a holiday that seemed to have gone wrong!

When the Wind Blows

A holiday in Dubrovnik. Dad had decided!

'We'll drive our car all the way and camp every night. There will be hundreds of miles of forests - and there'll be snow in the Alps. It's a long way but it'll be a holiday you'll never forget!'

'I've never even heard of Dubrovnik,' said Hannah. 'Can't we just go to Blackpool?'

'Yes, Blackpool,' agreed her brother. 'It was great last year.'

'No. This'll be a complete change,' insisted Mum. 'Different food, different people - lots of sunshine, and the Adriatic Sea, it will be like paradise.'

Secretly, she looked at the map, then at their battered old Volkswagen, and wondered if it really was such a good idea.

It seemed as though the summer term would never end. But, of course, it did. On the last day of July, with the car crammed full of baggage, they set off at last.

'We've a long way to go,' repeated Dad. 'But - I promise you - it'll be worth it! A week from now we'll be on a beautiful beach in Dubrovnik!'

Five days later, although the engine was making very strange noises, they were a thousand miles from home and still driving slowly on.

The children were staring impatiently out of the windows. They had crossed the snowy Alps and now there was nothing but dry grass and barren rock as far as they could see.

'Can't we stop?' Hannah groaned. It was getting late. She felt tired and hungry.

Mum looked over her shoulder.

'Don't worry. We'll find a campsite soon. And tomorrow we'll reach Dubrovnik and the sea!'

'I wish we were there now,' said Hannah gloomily.

'I feel sick,' said Carl.

'O.K. Let's stop at the next village. There's bound to be somewhere to spend the night.'

The road seemed to go on forever as it twisted higher and higher. When the children had almost given up hope, the car rounded a bend and there it was! A cluster of rough stone houses, a small café, a mosque and a slender, pointed tower - a minaret.

They swerved into the side of the road and stopped in a cloud of dust.

'At last,' gasped Carl. He flung open the door and fell out. Although it was late, it was still very hot.

Everyone trudged to the café, exhausted.

A wrinkled old man came out from the kitchen, swatting a large fly with his newspaper.

'I help, yes?'

Dad was startled. 'You speak English?'

'Yes. My grandson learn me. He good at school.'

'We're looking for somewhere to pitch our tent,' said Mum.

The man shrugged his shoulders.

'Picture ten?'

'No, we pitch our tent,' said Dad slowly.

The man still looked confused.

'Camping. Here. Tonight,' said Hannah.

The man threw down his newspaper and laughed.

'Oh, camping!' He paused, then walked to the door and beckoned. 'Come,' he said. 'Please. This way.'

Behind the café was a grassy slope where a goat was grazing.

'You like, yes?'

Dad nodded.

'Yes, perfect - thank you.'

The next moment a strong gust of wind caught his hat. It sailed into the air. He chased up the hill after it. The goat obviously thought it was a game and chased after it too.

Eventually Dad hurried back clutching his now half-eaten hat.

Strangely, the air was still again. The wind had dropped as quickly as it had come.

'Top of the field. That's the place to camp,' he said breathlessly. 'There's an amazing view.'

An old lady came through the gate. Her head was covered with a shawl.

'Be careful of the wind – it's called the Bora. In our village we call it 'The Goblin Wind'. It comes without warning. Sometimes it brings good luck - sometimes bad.'

'My wife's right,' said the old man. He pointed to some stony earth beside the café. 'Camp here. It is best.'

Dad hadn't stopped to listen. He was already hurrying back to the car to unload the tent.

'Come on. Don't hang about. Let's get the tent up before dark.'

The children followed him, pulled their enormous rucksacks from the car and struggled back through the gate. They dropped them on the ground.

'No, not there. The top of the field. Just follow me.'

But Dad,' protested Hannah.

'No buts. Just try to be helpful.'

The tent was old. It was also huge and heavy. When it was finally erected, Dad wiped the sweat from his face.

'You kids can put the pegs in. Mum and I will go down to the café and get water for the cooking.'

The goat watched them walk away. Then it wandered over. One of Carl's shoes was lying on the grass. It picked it up and ran.

'My shoe!' yelled Carl as he ran after it. 'Give it back!'

A few seconds later the air was filled with an angry roaring sound. It was 'The Goblin Wind' again - The Bora. The children froze with fear.

Hannah's hair blew in her face. In an instant she fell to the ground. She heard material flapping and ripping violently and glancing up saw the tent billowing above her. Half way across the field Carl crouched in the grass. His shoe didn't matter any more.

'The pegs,' he thought. 'We didn't put them in.'

He watched in horror as the torn remains of the tent swirled into the air. Mum and Dad came up the hill looking bewildered.

'The tent. Where's it gone?'

The children were speechless. They pointed in the direction of the village. In the fading light they could see it hanging limply from a rooftop.

'What are we going to do?' wailed Hannah. 'We're a thousand miles from home with nowhere to sleep.'

Through her tears she was aware of the old lady hobbling towards them. She was smiling.

'Come with me. You share our house. My husband, he makes the rooms nice now.'

The next morning when Hannah opened the shutters of their room, light came streaming in. It was already getting hot.

'Wake up, Carl,' she called. 'Come and see. It's fantastic out there.'

Chickens were pecking busily in the yard outside. A boy was filling a bucket from a pump. He turned and waved at her. Beside him, the goat waited patiently for a drink.

Carl yawned as he came to the window. Over the rooftops he could see range after range of mountains in the distance.

'The boy down there. He's pointing at something over to the right. I can't see what it is.'

He leaned as far out of the window as he could. Then he laughed.

'There are three men on a roof. I think they're rescuing our tent!'

The old lady appeared at the door.

'You come for breakfast now?' she asked.

Within minutes the children were rushing down the rough wooden stairs. Dad looked up and smiled.

'Mrs Stolac tells us that her grandson is waiting for you in the yard. He wants you to meet his friends. You can go swimming in the lake with them if you like. Tomorrow you can go riding the mountains.'

'And tonight there's a party in the village square,' said Mum. 'Everyone will be there - and we're the guests of honour!'

Mr Stolac walked in as they finished breakfast. He looked very pleased.

'My wife, her friends, they stitch your tent. It will be good.'

He was right. Although it took a week to mend, when they'd finished it was as good as new!

'I'm sorry we didn't get to Dubrovnik,' Dad said sadly, when it was time to leave.

'Who cares about Dubrovnik?' said Hannah. 'We've had a great time, haven't we Carl?'

'I'm glad,' beamed Mrs Stolac. 'As Moslems, we always help travellers when we can.'

'We'll never forget our new friends - or The Goblin Wind,' laughed Carl.

Thought for the day:
When something bad happens, remember - something good may be just around the corner.

Something to consider:
Have you ever been able to help someone when they were in trouble?

Axel was a boy in a foreign land. He was able to repay kindness in an unexpected way.

The Enemy

Jenny was out walking with her granddad.

'I'm going to show you something very special,' the old man said.

They wandered across a field until they reached a dip in the ground. It was overgrown with brambles.

'That's it,' he said. 'It might not look much but it's a lot bigger than you think.'
Jenny felt disappointed.

'So what's special about a big hole?' she asked.

'It's a bomb crater,' granddad said. 'That's what it is, and there are five more, over there.'

Jenny laughed.

'But that's silly. Why would anyone drop bombs in the middle of a field?'

'I'll tell you. It happened long ago, in the Second World War. That's what they should have hit.' He pointed at the village far off in the valley. 'It's an interesting story,' he said.

'Before the war, a German boy called Axel lived in the village. He was here to learn the language. All the local children liked him. He went to the local school and made lots of friends. Axel's Mum and Dad wrote him lots of letters from Germany. They arrived every week like clockwork.

Of course, everyone had heard of Hitler. We knew he was an evil and powerful man, that he was taking over Germany, frightening and bullying people. He was preparing for war.

Naturally, Axel's parents were worried. They wanted their son to come home to them. It was a sad day for us all when he left. I remember the bus leaving and all his friends waving goodbye. He said that he would write and that one day he'd return. But years went by and no letters arrived. We thought he'd forgotten us.

Then came the terrible shock. We heard that Britain and Germany were at war. Strangers arrived in the village, from London, looking very frightened, escaping the bombs. We made them as happy as we could. And other strangers too.

Mysterious scientists hid themselves away in the old rectory. We never knew who they were. It was all very secret. In spite of this, life still carried on in the village much the same as usual. Every day we heard terrible news of fighting and killing, but it all seemed far away.

No one dreamed that war might one day come to our peaceful valley.

'I'll never forget that night. I was sitting in the King's Head enjoying a glass of ale with my friends when we heard the plane.

It sounded a long way off and we didn't take much notice at first. But as the minutes went by the sound grew louder. We stopped talking and listened.

The pub door was suddenly flung wide open.

'That's a bomber - and it's right overhead,' yelled old Tom, as he fell into the room. One minute we were sitting there, talking about turnips, the next we were under the tables shaking with fear.

We waited and nothing happened. The plane was obviously going away. I laughed.

'We're stupid!' I said. 'Why would anyone drop a bomb on us? The sleepiest village in Dorset!'

As I crawled out from under the table, there were six deafening explosions. The whole building shook.

'Get out before it falls down,' I shouted. But of course it didn't.

We all groped our way home in the dark. I lay awake all night, expecting the plane to return.

The next morning we discovered that Frank Bower's field of turnips had been bombed! That was the only time war came to our village. We never heard an enemy plane again.

One day, a long time after the war, I was walking past the church when a car pulled up beside me.

A man got out. I thought I recognised him but couldn't be sure - until he spoke.

'Hello Mr Stewart,' he said. 'Do you remember me?'

He had a strong German accent. He looked very different to the boy I had known. But yes, it was Axel!

We walked to this field together and he spent a long time looking at these holes in the ground.

He seemed very pleased. 'I did that,' he said.

'I was shocked when I heard the order. My plane was to attack your village. Your scientists were working secretly - on something called radar! They had to be stopped. My job was to aim the bombs. It was a dark night and difficult. But suddenly, for a moment, I saw a light. Our plane was flying too high to be sure but it looked to me like the open door of the King's Head.

I waited another minute, then I pressed the button. The plane jerked as all our bombs dropped away.

'Right on target,' I yelled.

'Are you sure?' asked the pilot.

'Yes, I'm sure,' I said. 'We can head for home.'

My aim was perfect. We had bombed a field of turnips.'

Jenny sat quietly in the long grass.

She stared at the old man.
'Axel saved lots of lives, didn't he?' she whispered.
Granddad smiled.
'Yes,' he said. 'He was a true friend.'

○ ○ ○ ○ ○ ○ ○ ○ ○

Thought for the day:
It's easy to become prejudiced against people from other lands, especially if they speak another language.

○ ○ ○ ○ ○ ○ ○ ○ ○

Something to consider:
How can we get to know other people better?
Have you got a pen friend?

Chris was too worried about what other people thought of him.

The Winner

'Nothing but practice, practice, practice . . . and Sports Day's not for another two days yet,' muttered Chris.

He sat as far from the track as he could, watching as his class queued to run.

'Come over here Chris!' shouted Mr Symes. 'It's your turn next.'

Chris didn't move. He pretended he hadn't heard. His friend came over and sat beside him.

'That was my best time yet,' Tim said breathlessly. 'Half a second less and I'll beat the school record.'

Chris glanced at his watch.

'Ten more minutes and we can go home.'

'You haven't run yet. What's the matter?' his friend asked.

Chris shook his head.

'It's all right for you. You're the right shape for running. Just look at me.'

'You don't care what others think, do you?' said his friend. 'Just have a go and enjoy it.'

'And give the whole school a good laugh! No thanks!'

Tim shrugged his shoulders and delved in his pocket.

'Have a sweet,' he said.

Chris took one from him and studied it suspiciously. It was a small pink tablet.

'What is it?' he asked.

Tim grinned at him.

'I pinched them from my dad. Go on, give it a try.'

Chris hesitated.

'No thanks,' he said. 'It doesn't look like a sweet to me.'

'Go on,' said Tim. 'You're not scared, are you? It'll make you feel great. Honestly. I've had two today already!'

Chris put the sweet in his mouth and crunched it. It was very bitter.

'Don't chew it!' laughed his friend. 'Here, have another.'

Chris gulped and pulled a face. Suddenly a whistle blew. Mr Symes was coming over to them.

'Chris, you haven't run yet, have you? It's too late now. It's time to pack up. But don't worry. I'll make sure you have a chance tomorrow.'

By the time Chris reached home he was feeling on top of the world.

'Tim was right about those sweets,' he thought. 'They were revolting - but I'm walking on air. I feel amazing.'

He opened the back door and sauntered in.

Mum was in the front room, talking to someone on the phone.

'Hi Mum,' he called cheerfully.

Then he staggered. He screwed up his eyes and tried to focus them. He clung to the table. The room suddenly became blurred and started to spin.

'I'll just go to bed for a minute,' he whispered.

Mum had a nasty shock when she found him. He was sprawled at the bottom of the stairs.

'I'm O.K. Honest. Just need some sleep.'

That was what he wanted to say. But no matter how hard he tried, the words didn't sound right. When his mum phoned the doctor, she was close to tears.

'Please come quickly,' she pleaded. 'He's very ill.'

By the time he arrived, Chris was shivering violently and groaning. The doctor looked anxious as he examined him.

'I think he's swallowed something, Mrs Granger,' he said. 'You haven't left dangerous tablets lying around the house, have you?'

Chris's mum thought for a moment, then shook her head.

'Strange,' the doctor said. 'That's two boys with the same symptoms. Now don't worry. A couple of days in hospital should sort it out. You did the right thing calling me quickly.'

The school field was crowded with people. Sports Day had arrived. The first race was about to start when Mr Symes noticed Tim and Chris approaching across the field.

They came over to him very slowly.

'Out of hospital already?' he said. 'I didn't expect to see you two here! You're not fit enough to run, are you?'

'No sir,' said Tim in a shaky voice. 'But we'd like to watch.'

They went to the side of the track and sat down. An hour later, Tim turned gloomily to his friend.

'Hundred metres. I'd have won that easily,' he said.

Chris watched the runners lining up.

'My race next,' he said gloomily.

'But you didn't want to run,' said Tim. 'Now you've a good excuse.'

'That's right,' Chris muttered. 'I'd have come in last as usual. Who wants to be laughed at?'

But even as he said it, he was scrambling to his feet.

'Where are you going?' called Tim.

Chris didn't look round. He knew, if he didn't hurry he'd be too late.

Mr Symes looked surprised.

'You can't run,' he protested. 'You aren't well enough.'

'Please sir . . . I must,' Chris said.

'On your marks,' yelled a voice.

Chris's heart was thumping as he joined the other boys, crouched at the start.

'I don't care what anyone thinks,' he said to himself. 'They can laugh if they like.'

'Get set,' yelled the voice.

Every muscle in Chris's body tensed. He took a deep breath.

'Go!'

The runners bounded forward. Feet pounded the ground at a furious pace. It was the best race the crowd had ever seen. They shouted and cheered and shrieked and yelled. All eyes were on the leader, thundering towards the tape. As he crossed the line the noise was deafening.

Chris was gasping for breath.

Long after the others, he too crossed the line.

It was only then he realised, the cheering and clapping hadn't stopped - and no one was laughing. He felt confused. He couldn't understand it. The applause was especially for him.

Thought for the day:

Doing what you believe to be the right thing sometimes takes courage.

Something to consider:

Why do you think the crowd cheered Chris even though he came in last?

A boy in this particular story is faced with terrible danger. Perhaps everything will end happily. We can only hope.

Swimming for Frank

'Life isn't fair.' Jamie had said it so often.

Of course, his mum had always done her best. If he needed new trainers, he had them. She even bought him a new bike once although she couldn't afford it.

She worked at the local supermarket and was seldom at home when Jamie returned from school. As soon as he got in he'd switch on the TV. The programme didn't really matter. He just hated the silence of an empty house.

It had been fun when Alan lived next door, before he went to live in Newcastle. He was Jamie's best friend and they often played together on the waste ground at the end of their street.

'No brakes,' was their death-defying scream as they steered their bikes down narrow, twisting paths. Even when Jamie crashed to the ground and broke his ankle, he hid his tears behind a laugh!

It was a year now since Alan had gone. Newcastle was far, far away.

Of course, Jamie had other friends. Well, sort of. Lanky Smith and the rest of 'The Gang'. He'd known them for as long as he could remember. The other kids at school sniggered behind their backs and called them 'The Crazy Gang' - and with good reason. They always seemed to be in trouble. Jamie joined in. He pretended not to care.

That was all to change - suddenly - one frightening Saturday afternoon.

He was swinging on the garden gate when, behind him, the front door opened. He heard his mum's voice.

'I shan't tell you again,' she shouted. 'Get off that gate before you break it.'

'I'm bored,' Jamie growled.

His mum glared impatiently.

'Well you shouldn't be,' she said. 'Go out and find your friends.'

She disappeared back into the house and the door slammed. Jamie still swung on the gate.

'What friends?' he muttered.

He stared gloomily at nothing in particular. He was still deep in thought when the gang arrived. Five of them came round the corner of Mill Street on their bikes and rode towards him, squealing and whistling.

Frank Baker, who was in the lead, roared like a nuclear missile. With outstretched arms he hurtled past. Four more equally noisy missiles followed him, wobbling dangerously. Lanky was always last. His bike was far too small. His knees were almost knocking his chin as he pedalled desperately to keep up.

'Come on Jumby!' he yelled. 'On yer bike!'

Jamie, leaning over the gate, watched them all swerving from side to side as they went down the street. At the far end they turned and disappeared through a gap in the fence.

'Badlands, that's where they've gone,' Jamie said to himself.

He hurried to the shed, got out his bike and set off after them. It only took him a few minutes to get there but the gang was nowhere to be seen.

'The camp,' Jamie thought.

He knew that was where they would be. He pushed his way through the brambles. Sure enough, as he approached the hidden pile of timber and corrugated iron, he heard voices. Close by, the bikes were almost hidden in the long grass.

Suddenly there was silence.

Then urgent whispering.

'Hide them quick. Someone's coming.'

'Who is it? Can you see?'

'It's the police. I bet it is.'

'Well it's nothing to do with me. You bought the stuff, Frank.'

Jamie chuckled to himself.

'What's goin' on 'ere then?'

He tried to speak gruffly but it didn't fool Lanky.

'It's only Jumby,' he laughed. 'Come in mate. Have a fag.'

Jamie pushed his way through the narrow entrance. It was dark inside. The air was full of cigarette smoke. It smelt strange.

'Try this first. It's great stuff,' said Frank.

'No. I'm fine thanks,' said Jamie.

'Don't be a wimp. Go on. Have a sniff.'

Jamie took the glue can from him and held it to his nose.

'Go on then. Don't be scared.'

Jamie breathed in deeply.

'More. Go on. Sniff it up. That's not enough.'

It seemed as though the voice was far away. Jamie's head started to swim and, lost in a confused fog, he breathed in yet again.

He felt a mind-blowing sense of happiness - but mixed with a terrible fear. He heard laughter as he fell backwards, writhing and groaning.

How he got home, he couldn't remember. When he walked into the kitchen, his mum gasped.

'Jamie, what's wrong? Are you ill? Your face looks as white as a sheet.'

Jamie tried to smile.

'I'm O.K. Mum. Just tired.'

'You go and lie down,' she insisted. 'You're ill. I'm getting the doctor.'

'No, don't. I'm all right. Honestly Mum.'

'Get some sleep, then we'll see how you feel,' called his mum as he climbed the stairs.

By the next day Jamie was back to normal. As he walked to school, Lanky caught up with him.

'Have you heard about Frank?' he asked anxiously.

'No. What about him?' replied Jamie.

'He's in hospital. They say he might even die. Some pill he swallowed, they think.'

The two boys walked most of the way to school in shocked silence.

'Have you heard about Frank?' asked a boy in the playground.

Jamie just nodded. It was weird. He didn't even like Frank so why was he close to tears?

That evening Jamie ran home from school.

'Mum, I want to go swimming. Can I go tonight?' he pleaded.

His mum eyed him suspiciously.

'I suppose so,' she said. 'But I thought you didn't like swimming.'

Jamie looked thoughtful for a moment.

'They were talking about drugs at school. Next week there's a sponsored swim to help kids like Frank Baker. I need to practise.'

Thought for the day:

If your friends take drugs, it takes bravery to say no.

What's your opinion?

Was Frank really one of Jamie's friends?

We're free to make our own choices in life. The boy in this story took too much notice of his friend - and wished he hadn't!

The Vampire

Dad's bottle of special Scotch Whisky.

Oscar watched in horror as his friend opened it. He wouldn't drink it, of course ... He wouldn't dare, would he?

'Don't Phil,' he pleaded. 'It's my dad's. Please. He'll kill me.'

Philip laughed. 'Keep calm. Just a taste - that's all,' he said.

He raised it to his lips and took a very large gulp. Immediately, he started coughing and spluttering.

'Wow! Strong stuff,' he gasped. 'Try it! Go on - you must!'

Oscar shook his head.

'No thanks. Enough's gone already.'

'Don't be scared,' said his friend. 'We'll top it up with water. No one will notice.'

Oscar hesitated. He cautiously sipped. It tasted revolting.

'Go on! More than that! Don't be pathetic.'

Oscar put the bottle to his lips again and drank . . . and drank.

His eyes were watering and he thought he would be sick. Fighting for breath and with the world starting to spin, he put the bottle back on the table.

His friend was rubbing his eyes. They didn't seem to be focusing properly.

'Not feeling well,' he complained. 'I'm going home.'

Oscar went to the door with him, then returned and slumped onto the sofa. The T.V. was on.

A muffled, far away voice was announcing that the price of cigarettes was going up again, a man had spent ten hours stuck in a lift . . . and there was a vampire on the M4 motorway. It was causing serious problems.

Oscar sat up with a start.

'A vampire?' he thought. 'That's terrible.'

He dozed for a few moments, then woke up again. He found himself staring at the half-empty bottle. Suddenly he felt frightened.

'What shall I do? Dad will go mad when he sees it. But it wasn't my fault.'

He hid the bottle in the darkest corner of the broom cupboard, then staggered upstairs to bed. He still felt very ill.

When his parents arrived home, they found him fast asleep.

Next morning Dad poked his head round the bedroom door.

'Time to wake up,' he called. 'It's getting late.'

A confused face peered out from under the bedclothes.

'What? Eh?'

'You can't have forgotten,' said Dad. 'We're going to the cup final . . . today. Come on. Hurry up.'

Ten minutes later, Oscar crept slowly downstairs to the kitchen.

'Are you feeling all right?' asked Mum.

'I've got a headache,' Oscar moaned. His head was throbbing. 'I hate whisky,' he thought.

Mum looked cross.

'You've got a headache because you stayed in bed too long. I've told you before.'

Dad finished his piece of toast and stood up. 'I hope you're ready,' he said anxiously. 'We must get going. The M4 will be really busy today.'

Oscar's brain started racing. What had he heard about the M4? What? Gradually it came back to him.

'Dad . . . it was on the news. There's a vampire on the motorway so we'll have to take a different road.'

Dad laughed loudly.

'A vampire? You've been dreaming. Too many scary videos - that's your trouble!'

Oscar tried to protest but his dad wouldn't listen.

'Come on!' he said. 'Get your shoes on. We should have left ages ago.'

He hurried out to the car and started the engine.

Of course, they used the motorway. It was fast in spite of heavy traffic.

'A vampire on the M4 . . . ' Dad couldn't help laughing every time he thought of it.

Oscar sat quietly in the back of the car. He was starting to feel a lot better.

'Perhaps Dad was right,' he thought happily. 'It was just a stupid dream.' But then he looked uneasily at the traffic.

It was slowing down.

Finally, it ground to a halt. They waited . . . and waited.

Oscar craned his neck. All he could see was a queue of cars stretching far away into the distance. Now and again they crept forward but at a snail's pace. Dad was clicking his tongue impatiently. He glanced at his watch.

'We're too late for the cup final,' he said irritably. 'There's no way we can get there now.'

He was smouldering with rage.

Time went by.

Eventually, a policeman came by on his motorbike. He stopped to unbutton his jacket. He was hot and tired. Dad leaned out of his window.

'Excuse me, officer,' he called. 'Can you tell us what's wrong?'

'You didn't hear the news? A really bad van fire. It's caused chaos.'

Dad turned round slowly and glared at his son.

'A van fire... or a vampire?'

You'd have to be incredibly stupid - or drunk - to make a mistake like that, wouldn't you?'

Thought for the day:

It might seem exciting to experiment with alcohol but as a result we can look very silly - and feel horribly ill. Is it worth it?

Something to consider:

Many grown ups drink alcohol. Their bodies have matured enough to cope with it - providing they drink a sensible amount.

If we drink too much we lose control of what we do and what we think. This can bring many dangers, can't it?

Sometimes it's easy to forget the magic of the world around us. The children in this story needed to be reminded.

The Magic Stone

Ruth pulled a face.

'I hate walking,' she said. 'It's boring.'

'Can't we stay at home?' her sister asked. 'All we want are our Easter Eggs and a good video.'

'No you can't,' Dad answered. 'Granddad wants to go. We only see him once a year and he's looking forward to it.'

'What's the matter?' Mum asked when she walked in.

'Do we have to go?' Amy pleaded.

'Lydeard Hill's so steep, Granddad will take hours walking up there - and he wants to walk all the way to Triscombe. It's miles,' said Ruth sitting down and looking annoyed.

Just then, Granddad poked his head round the door.

'You'll have an amazing time. I can promise you that!' he said.

'I don't think so,' muttered Amy.

It took an hour to reach the car park at the bottom of Lydeard Hill. As soon as they got there, the twins, who had been squashed in the back of the car, tumbled out and rushed off up the winding path.

'You might find an ice cream van when you get to Triscombe,' called Granddad.

'I haven't any money,' gasped Ruth as she ran.

Her sister shook her bag.

'No problem. I've got plenty.'

'Slow down. Wait for us,' shouted Mum.

'Let them go. The path's safe enough,' said Dad. 'But Granddad, an ice cream van in a lonely place like Triscombe? What made you say that?'

Granddad smiled knowingly.

'Of course there wouldn't be, would there? That was silly of me!'

'We've left them miles behind,' said Ruth.

She looked back. In the distance she could see the path they had followed, snaking down Bagborough Hill and away through the trees. There was no sign of anyone. Her sister sat down on the grass beside her. She looked very hot.

'Why don't we slow down a bit? What's the rush?'

'Vanilla and butterscotch ice cream!' laughed Ruth. 'Come on!'

She pulled her sister to her feet.

'I'm dying for a chocolate flake,' said Amy.

Off they went again, even faster than before.

Meanwhile, Mum, Dad and Granddad plodded steadily on behind them.

'Can you see them yet?' asked Mum.

Two hours had gone by since they set out and she was feeling anxious.

'The Triscombe Stone's just at the top of the next ridge. They'll be there. I can't wait to see their faces. I think they'll be cross with you, Granddad.'

He looked indignant as he paused at the side of the path.

'Cross with me? Why?' Then he grinned. 'I think I've gone far enough,' he said. 'I'll see you back at the car.'

He turned and marched briskly back down the hill.

When the twins saw Mum and Dad coming, they ran to meet them. They looked furious.

'Where's Granddad?' asked Amy.

'He's gone back. I think he was tired,' said Mum.

'So where's the ice cream van?' Ruth demanded. 'He said it would be here.'

'And why come all the way up here anyway?' added Amy. 'There's nothing to look at but an old stone.'

'Nothing!' exclaimed Dad. 'Just look around you. Hills, valleys, forests. The view's incredible, isn't it?'

'And that's not any old stone,' said Mum. 'Did you touch it?'

'Why? It looks the same as any other to me,' said Amy.

'Didn't we tell you?' gasped Mum.

'Tradition says it has magical powers. Just touching it can make surprising things happen.'

'What sort of things?' asked Ruth suspiciously.

'Who knows?' said Mum.

'A magic stone? I don't believe it! Come on Ruth.'

Dad watched them chatting excitedly as they walked back down the hill.

'They wouldn't admit it but I think they're suddenly enjoying themselves,' said Mum.

Her husband looked thoughtful.

'How did you know about the stone?'

Mum shrugged her shoulders.

'I expect Granddad told me,' she said.

The twins were well on their way and had already reached the edge of Quantock Forest. Suddenly they noticed, in a wide clearing, something red and gold. It was shining in the sun. They ran over to it.

'It's an Easter Egg!' laughed Amy.

They sat down and examined it carefully. It looked delicious.

'What's it doing here? Someone must have dropped it,' said Ruth.

'Who cares? I'm starving,' said her sister. 'Let's eat it.'

Ruth stared into the trees. She could see something moving.

Amy saw it too.

'No,' she said in an absent-minded voice. 'We'd better show Mum and Dad first.'

'Look at that. It's incredible,' said Ruth.

A beautiful deer, with a small fawn close beside her, walked out from the shadows and came slowly towards them. The girls held their breath and kept perfectly still. They were so close. Suddenly the animals stopped. They gazed at the girls for some time. Then the deer put her head down and nudged the fawn back into the darkness of the trees. Amy dropped the egg into her bag.

'That was unbelievable,' she said to her sister as they made their way back to the path.

They were walking more quickly now as they descended through Bagborough Woods. It's strange how you sometimes know you're being watched. Amy felt it as she clambered over a stile. She hesitated and looked round slowly. She couldn't see anyone, but as she jumped down onto the path something caught her eye.

'It can't be,' she said. 'I don't believe it!'

There, hidden among the trees, was something blue, gold and shiny.

The twins raced over to it. Sure enough, it was another mouthwatering Easter Egg. They laughed loudly as they stared at it.

'The Triscombe Stone! It really works!' screamed Amy. She didn't say anything else.

For the second time she had a strange prickly sensation in the back of her neck. She knew she was being watched.

'Can you girls be a bit quieter?' hissed a voice in the shadows next to them.

Startled, they peered through the branches.

'Granddad!' whispered Ruth. 'What are you doing here?'

'A family of badgers, down below that bank,' he whispered back.

'Come closer and look - but ever so slowly. Not a sound.'

'I can see them,' breathed Amy. 'They're beautiful.'

They watched spellbound as the badgers hurried backwards and forwards, busily dragging fresh grass into the dark entrances of their set. The playful younger animals chased after them, pushing each other and rolling over and over down the slope.

For a long time, the twins crouched with granddad among the trees, hardly daring to move. Then, silently, they crept away.

'Thanks Granddad,' said Amy. 'That was real magic.'

Thought for the day:

We all enjoy the magic of film and TV but perhaps it's too easy just to sit at home and watch.

Something to consider:

Do you think you watch too much TV?

What could you be doing instead?

The boy in this story was too lazy to tidy up after the party. He didn't think about the consequences.

The Beast of Bodmin Moor

Holmes lived with the Baker family in a lonely cottage on the moor. To see him lying on his back on the floor, with his eyes closed and his legs in the air, you wouldn't have suspected he was clever.

Yet, although Holmes was only a dog, he would concentrate, listen to human conversations and think deep thoughts. And, of course, if Alice or David left the door open, this plump little Highland Terrier with very short legs would rush outside to investigate his exciting world.

One day, which Holmes would never forget, the children had invited all their friends around for a party. The nearest neighbours lived a long way off, but Mum and Dad had still warned them that it would be noisy.

And it was.

Holmes had shared in the excitement, running here, there and everywhere, diving under tables, barking, chasing imaginary cats and digging up the lawn to hide imaginary bones.

But when it was over and the guests had gone there was mess - as you would expect!

Scattered around the garden were dirty plates and glasses, Cola bottles - and even a half-empty can of hot dogs from the barbecue.

Holmes was sitting on the grass investigating the remains of a ham sandwich when he heard the children talking.

'Did you hear about the Beast of Bodmin Moor?' asked Alice. 'Molly Pritchard told me. Mr Skinner saw a huge wild animal in Lynn Valley. That's only three miles from here!'

Her brother sniggered.

'Beast of Bodmin Moor! Some people believe anything! Mr Skinner's eyes are so bad he can't tell the difference between a pig and a cow!'

'I'm so tired, I wouldn't know the difference either,' said Alice. 'Let's go back to the house.'

'Come on Holmes!' called David.

The dog glanced round uneasily. Then he chased after them.

The children wandered into the house and flopped down on the sofa.

'What's on TV?' asked David.

'Switch on and see,' yawned Alice.

'No you don't!' snapped Mum.

'Dad and I have done our share of the work. Now it's your turn. Go outside and gather up the rubbish.'

'What - now?' gasped Alice. 'I'm tired.'

'Yes, now - please,' said Dad. 'Before it gets dark.'

'And don't forget recycling,' said Mum. 'Plastic, paper and cans.'

They had hardly been in the garden ten minutes when David threw down his sack.

'Come on. That's good enough,' he said.

His sister glared at him.

'You haven't finished yet. Look at it all. In any case, it's not fair. I've picked up ten times as much as you!'

'You're stupid then,' he muttered. 'Just leave it. Do the rest tomorrow.'

Alice shook her head crossly as she followed him back to the house.

'That didn't take long, did it?' called Mum from the kitchen.

'No. It was easy,' answered David.

Later in the evening, Holmes - who had done his thinking for the day - was stretched out on the floor, dozing.

Suddenly he woke up, eyes wide open, every muscle tense. He pricked up his ears and listened intently. Was that a strange howling he had heard in the distance? He put his head on one side. It helped him to concentrate. No. Not a sound.

'Probably just a dream,' he thought. 'But perhaps I'll investigate.'

He went to the door and scratched at it.

'The dog wants to go for a run,' called Dad. 'Alice, take him in the garden will you?'

Alice looked outside. It was very dark.

'The Beast of Bodmin Moor might be out there,' she said.

Dad laughed.

'Nonsense! The only Beast is in Molly Pritchard's imagination! Just take Holmes for a quick run and don't be silly.'

'Come on Holmes,' she said. 'Don't be scared.'

The dog looked at her uneasily. Then he ran into the night.

'Holmes, where are you?' Alice called. 'Come back here.'

She could just make out the black shapes of bushes and trees as she placed one foot slowly in front of another. Suddenly she felt frightened. She could hear strange howling sounds somewhere in the wilderness at the end of the garden. Then there was a yelp and frantic barking!

A small, dark shadow raced towards her. She knew it was Holmes. Still barking, he rushed past. She turned and followed, running and stumbling, her heart pounding. The kitchen light guided her quickly home.

As she fell through the door, her father was crouching over the panting, shivering dog.

'What's happened?' Dad asked. 'Poor Holmes is terrified.'

Alice struggled to get her breath.

'There's a creature out there. I could hear it.'

He smiled reassuringly.

'Calm down. I'll get a torch. One thing's for sure - it's not the Beast of Bodmin Moor.'

Alice and Holmes looked at him doubtfully.

Mr Baker crept through the garden, swinging his torch from side to side.

'It's all right Holmes,' whispered Alice. 'There's no need to be frightened.'

'What's going on?' hissed David as he hurried after them.

"The Beast of Bodmin Moor,' said his sister. 'It's here in the garden. It nearly caught Holmes.'

David gulped.

'We'd be safer in the house, wouldn't we?'

Then, suddenly, they heard it. Not exactly a squeal. Not exactly a howl. Not very loud either. Somewhere in the darkness.

'Dad, what is it?'

David's voice was shaking.

His dad directed the light to penetrate the nearest bush. He gasped.

'There it is! I can see it!'

He dropped the torch and rushed back towards the house.

'I need protection! Thick gloves! Whatever you do, don't let it escape!'

Alice picked up the torch. The dim light illuminated the back end of a small, confused hedgehog. It was caught in the hotdog can from their barbecue.

Muffled, frantic noises were coming from inside.

'Poor thing,' cried Alice.

'Don't worry,' said David. 'We'll soon set you free.'

Holmes sniffed at the tin cautiously.

He was a clever little dog. He thought long and hard.

'We've caught the Beast of Bodmin Moor,' he decided. 'But how?'

Of course, Alice and David knew and they felt very guilty.

Thought for the day:

Humans and animals all share one world. It's up to each of us to keep our environment safe.

Something to consider:

The way we live creates so much waste and rubbish. Is it really necessary?

In this story the children's aunt had something to learn!

Jumping for Joy

Holly ran into the house.

'There's a plague of frogs in the garden! That's eleven I've seen today.'

'And I've seen thirteen,' said her brother. 'They must have come from the pond next door.'

'Whatever you do, don't tell your great aunt,' whispered Dad. 'She hates anything like that. We're relying on her to look after the cats, but she won't stay in the house if she finds out.'

'And that would mean no holiday,' said Michael anxiously.

At that moment the door swung open and there she was. An old lady with her grey hair in a bun. Aunt Joy.

'It's a really warm day,' she said. 'I'm going to sit outside to do some sewing.'

She opened the back door and disappeared into the garden. The children stared at each other.

'Frogs are everywhere,' said Michael. 'We must do something.'

'But what?' thought Holly. Glancing through the window, she could see her aunt sitting on the garden bench.

'How can we get her back in the house? Come on. We must talk to her.'

Aunt Joy looked up as the children crossed the lawn.

'What mischief are you two up to?' she asked.

They wandered over to her and sat down.

'Nothing,' said Michael.

'It's hot, isn't it?' said Holly. We don't think you should sit in the sun.'

'Very sensible,' said Aunt Joy. 'But I'll be all right. I've plenty of sun cream.'

Michael was thinking desperately.

'There are ticks in the grass. If one gets on your leg, you could be really ill. I'm sure I saw one just now.'

His aunt smiled.

'Thanks for warning me, Michael. I certainly wouldn't see them without my glasses.'

'So would you see something bigger . . . like a frog?' he asked.

'Only if it was really close. But then I'd die of shock. Frogs, toads, snakes - I loathe them all.'

Holly wasn't listening. Something was moving in the grass near her aunt's feet. To her horror, she realised it was a frog.

Suddenly it sprang upwards. It was an Olympic jump for such a tiny creature. Holly's heart was in her mouth as she watched it sail through the air. Beside her aunt was the open sewing bag.

Holly gasped as the frog fell in.

By pure luck, Aunt Joy was threading a needle at that moment or she would surely have seen it.

'I can't stand cold, slimy things!' she muttered.

Holly couldn't take her eyes off the bag. She didn't know what to do. It seemed an eternity before Aunt Joy looked at her watch.

'It's getting chilly,' she said. 'I think I'll go in and read for a while.'

She picked up her bag. Holly tried to snatch it from her.

'I'll carry it,' she said hastily.

'You're very helpful - but I can manage.'

She walked briskly back to the house. The children watched her climb the stairs.

'What's the matter?' whispered Michael.

'You didn't see?' hissed Holly. 'There's a frog in her bag. If it jumps out she'll die of fright.'

They sat on the sofa waiting for something to happen.

'Perhaps it slipped out without you noticing,' whispered Michael.

But he had hardly finished speaking when there was a frightened squeal upstairs.

'She's found it,' gasped Holly. 'Now there'll be trouble.'

They listened as the minutes ticked by. 'I wonder if she's all right,' said Michael. 'It's horribly quiet. We'd better go and see.'

Michael stood at the bottom of the stairs and watched his sister climb to the landing. Then, suddenly, Aunt Joy flung her bedroom door open.

'Just look at this!' she said, holding out her hand. On it was a small frog. It was croaking happily. 'I was reading my book and suddenly, there it was, right beside me.'

'But I thought you hated them,' protested Holly.

'So did I,' laughed Aunt Joy. 'It was a very nasty shock at first. But the more I looked at it, the more I realised, it isn't just a cold, slimy thing. It's a beautiful creature, isn't it?'

Thought for the day:

The more we study the world around us, the more wonderful we see it to be.

Something to consider:

Have you a favourite animal?

Are there any you dislike - and can you say why?

Thoughtless behaviour landed the boys in this story in more trouble than they expected!

A Voyage of Discovery

Reflected in the water, even the old chemical factory didn't look so ugly. The sun was shining and there wasn't a cloud in the sky.

On the riverbank, a boy with ginger hair and freckles got to his feet and yawned.

'So what shall we do now then?'

His friend tilted his head back and drank thirstily. Then he tossed the empty can into the river and searched around for a stone to throw at it.

The splash startled a family of ducks. Complaining noisily, they paddled quickly away.

'This'll really scare them,' cried Ginger.

He picked up an old brick, took a deep breath and heaved. It spun slowly through the air before plummeting down. A rowing boat was moored close by. He hadn't intended to hit it and was quite surprised when he heard the loud thud.

'Good shot!' laughed Bruce.

They raced along the bank to have a look. The brick hadn't caused any damage but the old boat certainly needed a coat of paint. Ginger gazed at it thoughtfully, then turned to his friend.

'It's just rotting away. No one's used it for years,' he said. 'So why not?'

As he scrambled into the boat, he grabbed Bruce's arm to steady himself.

'What you waiting for?' he asked, looking up. 'Scared?'

Bruce glared fiercely. Without saying a word he put one foot into the boat. Immediately, he lost his balance and fell heavily.

'Idiot! You'll tip us over!' Ginger shouted.

Then he noticed the riverbank. It was suddenly out of reach. The gap was widening rapidly. They were being carried away, caught in the grip of a strong current.

'What are we going to do? There's only one oar,' Bruce cried as he peered over the side.

'Just pass it to me,' Ginger snapped irritably.

But the oar was long and heavy. As he struggled with it, he almost let go. The blade plunged deeply into the water. He heaved and the boat swung round. The more he tried to control it, the faster it spun.

Round ... and round ... and round.

'It's no good. Stop rowing,' begged Bruce. 'I'm feeling sick.'

He helped to get the oar back into the boat. Then they sat glumly staring at the river as they drifted away.

'Mum will kill me,' Bruce said. 'I should have been home by now.'

Ginger sighed.

'Me too,' he said. 'My mum thinks I'm at the library.'

He suddenly pointed ahead.

'Look at that swan. Something's wrong with it.'

They watched it flapping its wings violently and hooting. It was struggling frantically to free its leg from a rusting supermarket trolley, dumped in the water. The boys stared at it until a bend in the river hid it from view.

They turned to look ahead and saw a small motorboat racing towards them.

'You need help?' shouted a man as he came closer.

He stood up, swinging a coil of rope.

'Catch it. I'll give you a tow,' he commanded.

By the time they reached a small landing stage, it was getting dark. They scrambled out as fast as they could.

There would be some explaining to do when they got home.

'You were lucky,' the man said. 'The boat looks so old, I'm amazed it didn't sink!'

They thanked him for his help and were about to dash away. Ginger hesitated.

'Could you phone the RSPCA?' he asked.

'Someone dumped a supermarket trolley in the river and a swan's caught its leg in it.'

'I'll phone them now,' said the man. 'Some people just don't think - and look at the trouble they cause!'

The boys nodded sheepishly. Then they ran like the wind.

Thought for the day:

It's easier to see other people's faults than our own.

What's your opinion?

Why do you think the story is called 'A Voyage of Discovery'?

Mary thought a day fishing by the river would be boring.
Perhaps she was wrong!

Gone Fishing

Mary watched curiously as Gran carried her fishing tackle out to the car.

'Why do you go so often?' Mary asked.

'You're on holiday,' said Gran. 'So why not find out? Come with me one day.' She got in the car and started the engine.

Mary waved, then wandered back into the house. She found her dad pretending to read the paper.

'Dad, why does Gran go fishing?' she asked. 'She never catches anything.'

He opened his eyes and yawned.

'It doesn't seem right, does it?' he said. 'Only men go fishing.'

At that moment, Mum walked in.

'Did Dad tell you?' she asked. 'We've had a phone call. We must go to Liverpool on Wednesday to visit Uncle George. He's in hospital. I've spoken to Gran and she said she'll look after you.'

'And take you fishing!' laughed Dad.

Mary pulled a face. 'Boring,' she thought.

On Tuesday, Gran came downstairs clutching a rod.

'I'll let you borrow this,' she said to Mary. 'But take care of it. It was Granddad's favourite.'

'Thanks a lot,' gasped Mary, trying to sound excited.

'We'd better take some food,' said Gran. 'It'll be a long day.'

Mary groaned quietly to herself. 'Sitting by the river - doing nothing - getting stung by gnats. Yes, a very long day,' she thought.

On Wednesday Mum and Dad left early. Mary spent most of the morning slumped on the sofa watching television. Gran bustled around the house humming to herself.

'I've made you some sandwiches,' she announced at last. 'Come on let's get going.'

Gran chattered continuously - all the way to the river.

'Wind in the Willows,' she said, as they parked the car and struggled over the bridge. 'Toad and Mole and Badger - and Ratty? You've read the book - of course! Pure magic! Good old Ratty. He knew how to enjoy life, didn't he?'

Mary listened and nodded occasionally as they walked along the riverbank. She was weighed down with hat, coat, net, rod, folding chair - and even a sun shade.

'When are we going to stop?' she pleaded.

'Nearly there,' Gran called as she hurried on. 'I know the perfect spot.'

Mary muttered crossly to herself as she followed.

'Here we are,' Gran called.

By the time Mary caught up with her, Gran had already unfolded her chair and was rummaging in a huge canvas bag.

'No time to waste. Let's get down to business.'

Five minutes later, the two of them were poised on the water's edge, fishing rods at the ready.

'Now watch carefully,' commanded Gran. 'Swing the rod back . . . like this. Mind the tree branches. Then a nice sweeping movement, forward . . . like this.'

The reel spun, the line arched gracefully through the air, a gentle splash - and there it was, a bright red float bobbing gently in the water.

'Your turn,' she said.

Mary tried hard not to laugh.

'Haven't we forgotten something?'

'No,' said Gran. 'Everything's perfect . . . '

'Bait?' suggested Mary.

'No,' said Gran. 'Never use bait. Don't need it.'

Mary shrugged her shoulders, cast her line into the water and sat down. From time to time she glanced at Gran who was gazing happily at the opposite bank.

'We'll never catch anything,' thought Mary. 'So what's the point of sitting here?'

'Just be still,' whispered Gran.

At that moment a luminous blue-green dragon fly skimmed over the water.

'Did you see that?' Mary asked.

Gran nodded.

A curious little insect was approaching Mary's float. She pointed excitedly.

'It looks as though it's rowing a boat!'

Gran smiled and nodded again.

'A Water Boatman. That's its name,' she whispered.

Just beneath the surface, a large silvery fish stared up at them curiously. Then a small face appeared in the shadows of the opposite bank. The creature slipped quickly into water and swam off.

'A water vole,' said Gran.

Later in the afternoon, two boys wandered along the footpath. They stopped and sat down on the grass.

'How's the fishing?' they asked.

'Never been better,' Gran said.

Suddenly the tallest boy pulled a camera from his bag.

'A kingfisher. Over there, under the trees. See it?'

He raised the camera slowly - and click.

'That should make a good picture,' he said.

'It's getting late,' said his friend. 'We ought to be going.'

'See you soon,' called Mary as they walked off.

Gran started winding in her line.

'We must go too,' she said. 'The end of another successful day.'

'Did you catch anything for tea?' asked Dad when they got home. 'No? Didn't think you would.'

'Never mind,' said Mum. 'You won't have to go fishing again.'

Gran smiled at Mary and winked.

Thought for the day:
If we look carefully at the world around us, we can appreciate it in surprising ways.

Something to consider:
When some boys asked Gran 'How's the fishing?' she said, 'Never been better!'
She hadn't caught anything, so what do you think she meant?

Something very special and exciting exists in Cornwall. The Eden Project. It's a collection of greenhouses – giant bubble-like structures – so enormous that you can spend hours inside, exploring steaming jungles and rain forests. Perhaps one day you'll have the chance to go there.

The children in this story were very lucky. They'd been looking forward to the trip for ages. At last they were on their way.

E.T.

'You said we were going to the Eden Project,' grumbled Judy as she stared out of the car window. 'So why do we have to visit Mr Turner?'

'Who is Mr Turner anyway?' demanded her brother.

'I've told you before,' said Mum. 'He's an old friend of ours. He said we must see his house before we go to Eden.'

'But why?' asked Judy.

'Very strange,' agreed Luke, grinning. 'His name's Edward Turner, isn't it? E.T. Extra Terrestrial.'

'Scary,' said Judy.

'Well, just remember to be polite - even if he's a monster with two heads,' said Dad. 'You'll meet him in a few minutes. That's his house.'

He pointed to an old stone cottage in front of them. The car pulled into the drive and they scrambled out.

The children were quite disappointed. He didn't have two heads. In fact there was nothing interesting about him at all.

'So what do you think of the house?' he asked.

'Nice,' Luke said. 'Yes, really nice.'

'And what about the view?' asked Mr Turner.

They walked to the window and looked out at the dismal valley. There was nothing but rock and dust everywhere and a line of huge lorries winding their way up a rough track from far below. There wasn't a tree to be seen. It was as barren as the moon.

'That's my quarry,' he said proudly. 'When I first bought it, the land was beautiful. You wouldn't believe it. Trees, grass, a stream - and all kinds of birds.'

Judy suddenly felt angry. She glared at him.

'Yes, it's a mess, isn't it?' he said. 'But what can we do? We all need stone - for houses, bridges, roads . . . by the way, I'm coming with you to Eden. I hope you don't mind.'

Just then Dad came into the room.

'It's time we were going,' he said.

The children should have been excited. Instead they were in a bad mood, knowing they would be squashed in the back of the car with Mr Turner.

'Why does that monster have to come?' they thought.

The road twisted and turned as it climbed into the hills. They didn't have far to go but the journey seemed to last for ever. Then suddenly, they rounded a corner and there it was. A huge sign.

'WELCOME TO THE EDEN PROJECT'

The car swung into the car park and Judy scrambled out.

'Just look at this!' she shouted.

Luke hurried over to her. They found themselves standing on the edge of the widest, deepest crater they could ever have imagined. Far below them, lines of people were following paths through the trees as they made their way towards huge, bubble-like structures gleaming in the sun. The children gasped. Mr Turner came and stood beside them.

'The Eighth Wonder of the World,' he said. 'Breathtaking, isn't it?'

Luke and Judy simply nodded. They were speechless.

'Space age greenhouses,' he said. 'Just one of them as wide as 35 football pitches and tall enough for the highest trees in the rain forest!

You know what used to be here? An old clay pit! Nothing but mud and diggers and lorries and noise - just like my stone quarry.

Who knows? With hard work, even my dusty old hole in the ground could be as beautiful as this, one day! You could help plan it, if you like.'

The children smiled at him. Perhaps he wasn't such a monster after all!

Thought for the day:

Humans must learn to live in harmony with nature. It's a challenge, but if we all try we can make a real difference to the world we live in.

Something to consider:

Humans have always caused problems in the world. But without plundering the earth for iron, stone, timber, oil, sand, clay - and an endless list of other things - how could we survive?

The Eden Project has been created to remind us that when we take from the earth, we must always find a way to pay back.

This boy found himself in serious trouble.
It was a moment that changed his life.

Buried Treasure

Chris dodged behind the shed. A stone hurtled past and landed with a thud.

'Missed!' he shouted.

Then he sprang from his hiding place, flung a stone back and waited. Will, grinning like a Cheshire Cat, peered round a bush. His arm jerked forward and another stone skimmed past Chris's ear.

'Right... it's war,' muttered Chris. 'This one will really scare him.'

He selected an extra large stone from the pile.

'Quite heavy,' he thought. 'A bit of extra power . . . a bit more height . . . and he'll run like a scared rabbit.'

His arm swung back. His muscles tensed, he aimed and the stone shot into the air. It climbed high over the fence, then plummeted down. Chris's heart sank into his boots.

'The window,' he gasped. 'Oh no!'

He waited for it. The sickening sound of shattering glass!

Crash!

Instantly there was a cry. Will came out of hiding, looking shocked.

'That was stupid,' he hissed. 'I'm going.'

He scuttled down the path beside the house - and disappeared.

Mr Cuthbert's furious face appeared over the fence.

'Haven't you any sense?' he snarled. 'I've warned you about throwing stones. Now look what you've done!'

Chris shrugged his shoulders. 'Sorry,' he blurted.

'Sorry? That's not good enough . . . I'll have a word with your mum. Right now.'

'You can't,' said Chris. 'She won't be home until late.'

There was silence for a moment. Mr Cuthbert was thinking.

'It had better not happen again,' he said. 'This is your very last chance. Come round now and help in the garden . . . work hard and I shan't say anything.'

Chris nodded.

'What do you want me to do?' he asked uneasily.

'I've six fruit trees to plant. You can dig the holes.'

An hour later, Chris knocked on his neighbour's door.

'You've not finished yet,' Mr Cuthbert barked. 'There's no way you could dig six holes that fast.'

'I've tried,' pleaded Chris. 'Really I have.'

Mr Cuthbert sighed impatiently.

'I'll come and look,' he said.

He marched to the bottom of the garden with Chris following nervously behind. Shaking his head crossly, Mr Cuthbert glanced into each hole.

'I can't plant trees in those,' he said. 'Nowhere near deep enough.'

'I'm sorry. I just can't do it. There's too much stone.'

Grumbling to himself, Mr Cuthbert got down on his hands and knees. He reached into a hole and scraped with his fingers. Then he looked up at Chris.

'No wonder you've had trouble,' he said.

He stood up and held out his hand.

'Look at these. You've hit something exciting.'

Chris stared at the small cubes of stone.

'What are they?' he asked. 'I've dug up loads of them already.'

'Then it's a good thing you stopped!' exclaimed Mr Cuthbert. 'You've discovered buried treasure!'

Chris laughed. 'No. They're just bits of stone.'

Mr Cuthbert was right. But it wasn't buried treasure of the kind Chris imagined. Under the soil was a beautiful mosaic pavement, part of a Roman villa abandoned and forgotten for fifteen hundred years.

Thought for the day:

There are many wonderful things in our world. If we look carefully enough, we can find them in most unlikely places.

Something to consider:

'I'm going to study to be an archaeologist,' Chris said.

With hard work perhaps he will. But what is an archaeologist?

Perhaps you can find out about some of these exciting people.

This story was inspired by an event in 1961 that changed the lives of people living on Tristan da Cunha, a tiny island in the Atlantic Ocean.

A New Beginning

Vicky wiped her face with the back of her hand. The air was getting unbearably hot. She picked up her bag, glanced round her room for a last time - and hurried from the house. Her mum was at the garden gate.

'The boat can't wait much longer,' she said.

'But what about Sammy?' cried Vicky. 'We can't leave without him.'

Mum didn't say anything. She just shook her head sadly.

Dad was struggling out of the front door with two enormous bags. His face looked tired and drawn. He hesitated for a moment, then slammed the door and came down the path.

Vicky was close to tears.

'Where's Sammy?' she pleaded.

'I've already told you,' he said. 'No animals. It just isn't possible. I'm sorry.'

At that moment the ground started to shake violently.

A powerful gust of wind sucked up the smoke to reveal tiny cottages nestling at the foot of the volcano. A door was suddenly flung open and Vicky's friend Luke and his parents fled across the burning grass.

'What are you waiting for? Come on!'

Vicky's dad sounded frantic.

She couldn't hear what he said next. The volcano was bellowing like a mortally wounded monster.

They picked up their bags and ran. When they reached the top of a steep gully, Vicky stopped and sat down. Her bag was heavy and she was gasping for breath. On either side were empty fields where sheep and cows had once grazed.

'I wonder where they've gone,' she thought.

'Come on Vicky,' shouted Dad urgently from deep in the gully.

'It's the last boat.'

Picking up her bag, she scrambled and slid down the winding, dusty path. At the bottom, she found her mum waiting anxiously on the rocks. Beside her, men strained on ropes to control the boat that rose and fell on the waves. Luke reached up and grabbed her bag.

'I'll take that,' he shouted. 'Now jump.'

A huge wave was carrying the boat towards her. She sprang.

At the same time she was aware of a dog standing on the rocks above. It was barking furiously.

Vicky squealed with delight as it leaped into her arms.

'Sammy,' she gasped. 'Where've you been?'

Her dad quickly sat down beside her.

'I'm sorry,' he said again.

Vicky hugged the dog tightly.

'You know we can't take him,' she thought he was about to say.

But he didn't.

There was a sudden rumble, then an ear-splitting explosion.

'The volcano - we must get away!' cried a frightened voice.

Men's strong hands gripped the oars.

'Heave . . . heave!' they cried.

Vicky stroked Sammy's head gently. Although drenched with spray she hardly noticed. She was straining her eyes, hoping to catch a last glimpse of her island home, now hidden by the smoke. Luke plucked at her sleeve and pointed.

'We're catching up with them. Look.'

There were four long-boats in front, all crowded with people and dangerously low in the water.

Beyond them, Vicky could see vast clouds of seabirds circling above the cliffs of Nightingale Island.

'Four hours and we'll be there,' shouted her dad above the roar of the wind. 'A ship is on its way. We'll be in England in a few weeks. You'll like it. The people are nice.'

But would she really like it?

Her dad had never been there - so how did he know?

Vicky tried to smile but she felt scared.

Thought for the day:

Immigrants come to our country for many reasons. The one thing they have in common is that they've been forced to leave their home and friends.

Something to consider:

Can you find Tristan da Cunha on a map?

Everyone on the island had to flee. You can see one of the small boats they used, at the Maritime Museum in Falmouth, Cornwall.

A volcano on the remote island of Tristan da Cunha suddenly erupted on 9th October, 1961. All the people living there fled for their lives. They reached Nightingale, an island only inhabited by sea birds.

Eventually they were rescued and came to England.
They were refugees.

Return to Paradise

Vicky was nine years old and had never been to school. Her parents and other islanders had taught her all that she needed to know. As she walked across the playground of a big London Primary School she was worried.

It was her first day. What would it be like? Would people be friendly - and what would they expect her to do?

Her mum had left her at the school gate.

'Don't come in,' Vicky had said. 'I'll be fine.'

But she had never seen so many children before. There were hundreds, and the noise was deafening. She stopped at the main door and stared up at the enormous building. Suddenly a teacher appeared with a girl beside her.

'Ah, Vicky,' she said. 'Mary's in your class. She's volunteered to show you round. It's a big school and you're bound to get lost!'

'Come on,' the girl said.

As they wandered off down the corridor, she glanced curiously at her new friend.

"You need to get a school uniform - and fast. The other kids will die laughing if you wear clothes like that!'

Vicky felt confused.

'Why?' she asked anxiously. 'What's wrong with them?'

'Nothing - if you lived two hundred years ago,' Mary said. 'There's no way you can walk around in those old things.'

They stopped and looked into a room. Vicky looked excited.

'I know what that is. A television.'

'So?' laughed Mary. 'Nothing unusual, is it?'

'Of course not,' said Vicky defensively. 'I saw one last week in a shop. We haven't got one in our flat - but there is a phone. It scares me to death every time it rings!'

'Where did you say you come from? The moon?' gasped her friend.

'Tristan,' said Vicky crossly. 'I've never seen a cinema, a bus, a train, a plane - or even a shop. But I don't care. It's better than being here.'

Vicky couldn't wait for lessons to end on that first day. She tried hard to understand, and Mary did what she could to help.

'It's hopeless,' Vicky thought. 'Nothing the teachers say makes any sense. I just want to go home.'

The bell went.

What a relief! School was over at last.

'Where did you say you're from?' asked one of the boys as they left the room.

'Tristan da Cunha,' she said.

'Where? Never heard of it!'

'Tristan where?' another boy sniggered.

Vicky hesitated.

'I live in Edinburgh. It's a little village - and a lot nicer than here,' she added.

'Edinburgh? A little village? She's got a screw loose in her head!' scoffed someone behind her.

'It's a city in Scotland. Don't you even know that?'

The gang of boys wandered away, pointing at her and laughing loudly.

'Why say you're from Scotland?' demanded Mary. 'Everyone knows Edinburgh's not a village - so why say it? People will think you're stupid.'

'I didn't say Scotland,' Vicky protested. 'Edinburgh is where I live. It's the name of my village on Tristan. It's by the sea - everyone's really nice to each other - and it's a lot better than living here.'

'Will you go back one day?' asked Mary.

Vicky looked as though she might cry. But she didn't.

'I hope so,' she said.

Thought for the day:

Most of the islanders returned to Tristan when it was safe but they had made many new friends in Britain.

Something to consider:

Even when something terrible happens, it's possible that some good may come out of it. There is an old saying that 'every cloud has a silver lining'.

Can you find Tristan da Cunha on a map?

This story is based on the author's experiences in 1963, long before the Falklands War. A long sea voyage was the only way to reach the islands.

A New Island Adventure

Mr Stephens came home one day and said, 'I've got a new job - looking after a farm on an island.'

His children stared at him blankly.

'Where?' asked Josh.

'It's called New Island,' said Dad.

Emma eyed him suspiciously.

'I've never heard of it. Is it far away?'

'It's not exactly close,' he said.

Then he hesitated.

'It's one of the Falkland Islands. I'll show you where it is.'

Mr Stephens went to the cupboard, found a map and spread it out on the table. He searched for a few minutes, then drew a cross with his pencil.

'There,' he said.

Josh peered over his shoulder.

'But Dad,' he gasped. 'It's so small, it's not even marked on the map.'

'And just look where it is,' wailed Emma. 'It's almost in the Antarctic. It's thousands of miles away. We don't have to go - do we? What about our friends?' she pleaded.

'You can keep in touch with them - and I'm sure you'll find plenty of new ones.' He paused before adding, 'Of course things will be a bit different.'

The children never forgot those words. Different? He was certainly right about that! They had seen so many changes since their mum died. So it wasn't surprising that they were thinking sadly of home as they neared the end of their long voyage.

They were standing on the heaving deck of a tiny cargo boat, shivering in the biting wind. It was better than sitting in their cabin, enduring heat, noise and sickening fumes from the engines. Suddenly the boat lurched sideways as, with a frightening roar, a huge wave swept across the deck.

Josh grabbed his sister's hand.

'Emma! Don't let go!' he shouted.

With water flooding past them they scrambled down a flight of steps and burst into the dining room. The door slammed behind them. A sailor was there with a jug, calmly splashing water over the tables!

'What are you doing?'demanded Emma as the ship lurched again and she fell against her brother.

He laughed.

'Plates don't slip on a wet tablecloth!'

Emma looked at the chairs, each now chained firmly to the deck.

'Dinner's in five minutes,' he said. 'You'd better tell your dad.'

'Not much point,' said Josh.

'Dad's in his cabin,' explained Emma. 'He's feeling seasick.'

The sailor nodded gravely.

'He'll be glad to have a few hours on dry land then. We call at Port Stanley tomorrow to refuel - and it'll be a beautiful day.'

The next morning when the children went on deck, they found the wind had dropped and the sun reflecting on a turquoise sea.

'Look,' shouted Josh. 'It's an island.'

They ran to the ship's rail and stared anxiously at the mysterious land that had appeared. By midday they were sailing so close to shore that they could see a solitary figure waving to them. He was standing on a beach of dazzling white sand.

An hour later the ship turned and a lighthouse came into view, perched on a rocky headland.

'We reach harbour in ten minutes,' shouted a sailor.

The heavy throbbing of the ship's engine now changed to a gentle purr. The Darwin slowed to manoeuvre cautiously through a narrow, rocky channel - and there before them was Port Stanley - a tiny cluster of white painted houses, encircled by mountains.

The children glanced round as their dad hurried on deck with a camera. His face still looked green, but he smiled.

'The Falkland Islands at last,' he said. 'A few hours ashore, then the last leg of the journey. We're almost there.'

A huddle of people stood on the beach watching curiously. Ropes were thrown, the engine fell silent and the ship drifted sideways to the quay. It was soon safely moored.

'I've business to attend to,' said Dad. 'You go off and explore. Just ask if you get lost - and don't go too far.'

'Ask who?' said Emma as they wandered through the deserted streets.

'Where is everyone?' exclaimed her brother.

The next moment an old Land Rover swung round the corner and rattled off up a rough track.

'You haven't seen Bruno, have you?' said a voice behind them.

The children turned and saw a girl with dark, curly hair scrambling over a fence.

'Yes - if Bruno's a fat little dog,' said Josh. 'I saw him about two minutes ago.'

The girl sighed.

'Never mind. He'll come back when he's hungry.

'You must be Josh and Emma - the New Island kids. We've all heard about you. You'll like it here. There aren't many of us - but we're really friendly.' She hesitated. 'A word of warning. William can be a problem. If he gets in the house he'll walk off with anything he can pick up.'

Josh looked indignant.

'Why not tell the police? They'll soon sort him out.'

'There aren't any police!' laughed the girl. 'In any case, you can't arrest a penguin.'

Emma and Josh looked at each other. They remembered Dad's words.

'Things will be a bit different,' he had said.

They felt a surge of excitement. Perhaps life wasn't going to be so bad after all!

Thought for the day:

Facing changes in our lives can be very frightening - but it can also lead to exciting adventures.

Something to consider:

Why not look for the Falkland Islands on a map?

New Island may be too small to find. It's a paradise for millions of penguins!

The girl in this story was looking forward to going on holiday – but then she had a nasty shock!

Scatter Brain

Mr Barret sat on the suitcase.

'It won't close,' he grumbled. 'There's just too much in it.'

'What did you say, dear?' called his wife.

She carefully placed one foot in front of another as she came down the stairs. In one hand she held a large case, in the other a beach bag. A pair of Wellington boots was tucked under her arm.

'Wellington boots? I thought we were going to Brazil to lie on a beach!'

'And so we are! I was just tidying up. They were in Emma's bedroom - what they were doing there, I can't imagine.'

Mr Barret grunted.

'How can anyone be so untidy and forgetful? Come to think of it, what's she doing? I bet she's even forgotten we're going today!'

'Don't worry, she's nearly finished packing. Sally from across the road is helping her.'

At that moment a girl wearing a swimming costume, a straw hat and sunglasses came into the room.

'How do I look?' she asked.

Mr Barret sighed impatiently.

'Very nice – but the taxi will be here in ten minutes. You're supposed to be ready to leave.'

'No problem, Dad. I shall be.'

Mum looked doubtful.

'You'd better check you've got everything. Most important, where's your passport?'

'Don't worry, it's safe. I just wanted to show Sally my awful photo!'

The door-bell rang. Dad glanced out of the window.

'It's the taxi,' he gasped.

'It can't be. He isn't due to pick us up yet.'

'The clock must be slow! Someone go and tell him to wait. I must get this suitcase closed.'

Emma was half way to the door when her mum stopped her.

'I'll deal with the taxi. You get changed and say goodbye to Sally. I want you down here and ready to go in two minutes!'

Emma fled upstairs in a panic.

'Sally, you'll have to go,' she screamed. 'The taxi's here.'

The journey to the airport was very slow. There was so much traffic on the road. Everything came to a complete standstill on the motorway for half an hour. Then the taxi crept forward, stopping, starting and stopping again.

'We should have left earlier. I did tell you,' said Mum. She studied her watch anxiously.

'There's plenty of time,' said Mr Barret, humming to himself quietly. 'At least, I hope so,' he thought as he stared at a traffic light that seemed determined to stay red.

When the taxi finally pulled up outside the Air Terminal, Emma flung the door open.

'We can't go anywhere until the baggage is out of the boot,' said Mum.

'Keep calm. There's no need to rush.'

'Are you booked on the midday flight to Rio de Janeiro?' asked the driver.

'Yes, we are,' smiled Dad happily. 'Why?'

'Because you're late. Last call for the flight was five minutes ago.'

Mr Barret's face turned as white as a sheet.

The driver sprinted to the back of the car and heaved everything onto the pavement.

'If you're quick you'll be in time. Good luck!'

As they struggled through the terminal door, Mrs Barret glanced at her daughter.

'Emma, use your brain for a change. Brazil's one of the hottest countries in the world - and you've brought a thick winter coat!'

'Don't fuss!' snapped Dad. 'We're not going anywhere unless we're fast.'

A smartly dressed lady at the check-in desk looked at their tickets.

'You're almost too late,' she said. 'And you shouldn't have so much hand luggage. I'll have to charge you extra.'

'Emma, most of it is yours,' said Mr Barret crossly. 'Just look at it all. You won't need half of it.'

'You really must be quick,' said the check-in lady. 'Show me your passports please.'

Mrs Barret could never explain how, but she had an uncanny way of knowing when things were going wrong. She looked at her husband.

'I haven't got the passports,' she said weakly. 'I left them on the kitchen table.'

'No you didn't,' chuckled her husband. 'I picked them up. Here they are.'

With a triumphant flourish he placed them on the desk.

The lady picked them up and studied them.

'I'm sorry, there are only two here. Unless your daughter has one, she can't travel.'

Emma felt sick.

'My passport. Where can it be? Sally had it last. What did she do with it . . . ? I know where it is. It's in a bag.'

But she had six bags of different shapes and sizes. Her dad stared at them uneasily.

'Which one? Tell me quickly or we'll miss the 'plane.'

'I don't know - but it's in one of them. I know it is. Nothing was left in my room. I checked really carefully before I came downstairs.'

'Help me get them open!' Dad shouted. 'Don't just stand there.'

Ten minutes later the floor was strewn with Emma's belongings. Mr and Mrs Barret, their daughter and even the smartly dressed check-in lady were on their knees searching. There was no sign of the passport anywhere. Her dad was in a rage. He held up a book. He glared at the title:

'How to Succeed Without Trying.'

'Emma, you've brought this - and forgotten your passport . . . '

He didn't know what else to say. There was an awful silence as everyone repacked the bags.

'No holiday,' said Mrs Barret tearfully. 'I was really looking forward to it.'

Emma had a lump in her throat.

'I'm sorry,' she whispered.

She put on her coat, sighed, stuffed her hands in her pockets and walked away. Her right hand touched a small, thin book. Her heart started pounding. It couldn't be. Could it? Sally wouldn't have put it there - would she?

Slowly Emma pulled the passport from her pocket. The check-in lady grabbed the phone. She talked earnestly for a while. Mrs Barret and her daughter couldn't hear what she was saying. They stood waiting, not daring to hope. Mr Barret's legs felt like jelly. He had to sit down.

Suddenly, the check-in lady looked at them. Then she smiled.

'The plane is about to leave. If you follow me you may just be in time.'

Thought for the day:

It's no good always relying on other people.
We need to take responsibility for our own actions.

Something to consider:

How did you leave your bedroom this morning? Why is it important to be tidy?

Lilly was a pretty girl. But although she was also very clever, she was impetuous. She did things on the spur of the moment, without thinking. Until, that is, one terrible day that she would never forget.

Red Head

'If only I had the money,' Lilly thought.

She gazed longingly at the make-up bag on the counter.

'The perfect Christmas Gift,' the label said.

Yes. It was exactly what she wanted.

'But Christmas isn't for ages. That's no use to me. I need it now.'

A tall, smartly dressed man was standing nearby, choosing a lipstick. Lilly giggled to herself.

'I don't think that colour really suits you,' she thought.

A woman with three small children squeezed past her, pushing her against the counter. The bag was right there. Under her nose. She stared at it.

'It's a small thing. There are so many of them. If someone took it, so what? They wouldn't miss it.'

Her hand crept closer. A quick glance around . . . Snatch!

One moment the bag was there. The next, it had gone.

With her hand in her pocket, she hurried to the shop door. She felt safe, being swept along by the jostling crowd. But then she became aware of a tall, smartly dressed man, not far behind her . . .

Her heart was thumping. She crossed the pavement, bumping into a woman. She was loaded with shopping.

'Sorry,' Lilly uttered.

Then she ran across the road and jumped on a bus.

'A narrow escape,' she thought.

But suddenly she felt frightened.

'I didn't really need it. I've never pinched anything before. So why?'

She tried to reason with herself.

'The store was crowded. No one noticed. They couldn't have. Could they?

The smartly dressed man . . . A store detective?

He wasn't really choosing a lipstick, was he?

He was so close. He must have seen. He'll recognise me . . . how could he forget my long blonde hair?'

Lilly started to panic as she jumped off the bus and raced home. To her relief, Mum was out. Still at work. The house was empty.

'I must do something - urgently,' she said to herself. 'But what?'

She ran to the bathroom and glared in the mirror.

'Lilly, what have you done? You're an idiot.'

She looked thoughtfully at her long, blonde hair. Suddenly she knew what to do. She opened the bathroom cabinet.

'Yes, that's the answer,' she muttered.

A bottle of hair dye. At the back of the shelf, where it had stood for longer than she could remember.

'Mum's never used it,' she thought. 'So she won't mind. And no one will recognise me - even at school. Gorgeous jet black hair. What a laugh!'

She carefully draped a towel round her shoulders. Then she opened the bottle, screwed up her eyes and bent over the wash basin. She took a deep breath.

'Well, here goes,' she said.

She emptied the dark liquid over her head and rubbed it in vigorously.

'How long should I leave it?' she wondered. 'Why didn't I read the label?'

When her mum arrived home, she heard desperate crying upstairs.

'What on earth's going on?' she muttered.

She rushed to the bathroom. For a moment she failed to recognise Lilly, her head still in the washbasin, her hair caught in a hopeless tangle round a tap.

'Help me! Help!' she wailed.

'There's only one thing I can do,' said her mum.

She quickly found some scissors and started work. Five minutes later, Lilly looked at herself in the mirror. She stared in horror.

Her face - and what was left of her hair - were brilliant red.

Thought for the day:

Whatever we do in life, think first. There are always consequences.

Something to consider:

Although Lilly only took something small, she knew she would be in serious trouble if caught. She vowed she would never steal anything again. She had learned her lesson!

Have you ever done something you've lived to regret?

The boy in this story couldn't be trusted.
He had a difficult lesson to learn.

Seal Island

Kevin stood on the quayside. He glared down at his dad working on his boat 'Water Witch'.

'Why can't I come fishing with you? Mum said I could.'

'It's simple, Kevin. I can't trust you to be sensible.'

'It's not fair,' said the boy. 'How am I going to learn to be a fisherman if you won't take me out?'

'You - a fisherman? Then you must be reliable and always do the right thing at the right time. If you can't be trusted, you're no help to anyone.'

'But Uncle Frank's not back yet from Penzance so you need me, don't you?'

His dad glanced at his watch and then looked thoughtfully at his son.

'Please, Dad,' Kevin pleaded. 'I'll be really helpful. I promise.'

'All right,' sighed Dad. 'It's getting late in the day so we'll just go to Seal Island. Then I can see how you get on. You never know, you might learn something.'

Half an hour later they left the calm water of the harbour and headed out to sea. Kevin was enjoying himself. He loved going to Seal Island - and sitting in the stern of the boat holding the tiller was his favourite job.

His dad, standing in the bow, waved to him and shouted. Kevin could hardly hear him above the steady roar of the engine.

'You're doing all right. Just hold course another minute, then come slowly to starboard. Steer north of Black Rock.'

Kevin nodded. 'Easy,' he thought.

He leaned back, closed his eyes and imagined himself on a huge yacht sailing single-handed to America. Alone at sea for weeks. Sails billowing. The Statue of Liberty to starboard. Crowds cheering. The fastest Atlantic crossing ever.

'Kevin!' bellowed his dad. 'Stop dreaming and think. I said slowly to starboard. Pull on the tiller quickly, or we'll sink.'

The boat had turned sideways to the waves and was keeling over dangerously. Kevin hung on and heaved. It took all his strength but the boat slowly swung round. He breathed a sigh of relief as it righted itself.

Moments later his dad shouted again.

'What are you doing? I said north of Black Rock. Not straight at it! I'll take over - before something really nasty happens.'

'What's the fuss? I wasn't doing that badly,' Kevin muttered sullenly as his dad ran towards him along the sloping deck.

But suddenly he stumbled forward with a cry of pain.

He got to his feet, rubbing his arm and looking furious.

'You know how to coil rope properly. So don't just throw it down for me to trip over.'

'Sorry, Dad,' said Kevin.

He went into the tiny cabin and pressed his nose to the window. The narrow creek on the west side of the island was getting steadily closer.

'Five minutes and we'll be there,' shouted his dad. 'If we cut the engine and drift we'll see plenty of seals.'

Kevin looked disappointed.

'What's the point in coming if I can't land?'

'All right, you've just got ten minutes. The tide's on the turn. Remember - it's a dangerous place - and a nature reserve. Think what you're doing - and don't disturb the seals. Any nonsense and I'm warning you - I'll go home without you.'

'Leave me alone out here? You wouldn't dare!' laughed Kevin.

'Don't you be so sure!' said his dad. 'Now, you see that flat rock? Jump when I tell you to. Take the rope and secure it to the iron ring.'

Kevin balanced in the bow, clutching the rope and poised to spring.

'Now!' shouted his dad.

It was easier than the boy expected. The rock wasn't slippery - it was the only one not covered in seaweed. He tied the rope firmly, then clambered higher. Seals were lying everywhere in the sun. Kevin laughed. They looked so helplessly fat. He clapped his hands and screamed at them.

'Stupid animals!' he shrieked. 'This is my island. Go away!'

It took some time before he realised that the noise of the boat engine had changed. It had roared for an instant. Now it was rapidly becoming quieter. Kevin gasped with horror. The boat was already out of the creek and disappearing from view.

'Dad! Come back! Don't leave me. Please!'

His dad didn't seem to hear.

Kevin sat down on a rock and sobbed quietly.

'Why?' he asked himself. 'I know he warned me - but he wouldn't really leave me here. Would he? He'll come back in a minute.'

But time went by. The sun got lower in the sky and it started to get dark. Huge, grey shapes were slowly creeping over the rocks. The seals had returned. He felt lonely and frightened.

'What's going to happen to me? Do the right thing at the right time. That's what Dad said. But what is the right thing?'

He shivered. It was getting cold.

'I must hurry . . . further from the sea . . . some kind of shelter . . . perhaps even a dry cave.'

He scrambled to his feet and picked his way carefully inland. Shadowy shapes were moving all around him.

'It's all right, seals,' said Kevin trying to sound calm. 'Nothing to worry about. It's only stupid, useless me.'

'Stupid, yes - but I think you're learning,' said a voice. 'And never say you're useless.'

Kevin was rooted to the spot. The voice sounded familiar! It couldn't be. But then it couldn't be a seal either!

Kevin strained his eyes to see in the blackness.

'Dad?' he whispered cautiously.

'Sorry, son. I shouldn't have frightened you. But perhaps you've learned a lot of things tonight. Most important, remember what I said about trust?'

A hand firmly grasped Kevin's arm to guide him round a large rocky outcrop. Staring into the darkness Kevin could just make out the shape of 'Water Witch' floating on a beautifully calm sea. It was the most wonderful sight he had ever seen.

Thought for the day:

If you want to earn people's trust you must be responsible for your actions.

What's your opinion?

Kevin thought he had been abandoned. Do you think his dad did the right thing?

Dan was a greedy boy. He was in for a shock!

Consequences

'A mouse has been in the cupboard!' shrieked Mrs Watson.

She was clutching the remains of a packet of marzipan. The end was torn open and most of it had gone.

'I needed that for the Christmas Cake,' she sighed. 'I'm sure it was a mouse. Just look at the teeth marks.'

Her husband took the packet from her and examined it. The kitchen door opened slowly behind him.

'Dan . . . ' growled Dr Watson, without looking round.

'You like marzipan . . . don't you?'

'It's quite nice,' Dan said cautiously. 'Why?'

'Because someone's been eating it.'

Dan grinned.

'Sorry,' he said.

'And you still haven't cleaned out the rabbit hutch,' Dr Watson added crossly. 'I shan't tell you again.'

'I'm tired of grumbling,' sighed his wife as Dan left the kitchen munching a biscuit. 'He takes things without asking - and just doesn't seem to care.'

Later that evening Mrs Watson nudged her husband, who had fallen asleep in front of the fire. He woke up with a startled snort.

'Eh? What?' he stammered.

'Let's go to the market tomorrow and buy a Christmas tree,' she whispered. 'It's just what Dan needs.'

'You can't be serious,' Dr Watson protested. 'He doesn't deserve it.'

'Oh yes he does!' his wife laughed. 'Just you wait and see.'

The next day they went to the market but Dr Watson was in no hurry. By the time they got there, only one tree was left.

'It's far too big,' he said. 'We'll never get it in the car.'

'I'm sure you'll manage somehow, dear,' smiled his wife.

In the evening Dr Watson went into the garden. After planting the tree in a bucket, he dragged it to the house.

'This is ridiculous,' he thought irritably as he struggled to get it through the door. When Dan came downstairs he followed a trail of earth and pine needles into the front room. His dad was on his knees with a dustpan and brush.

'It's great - just great,' Dan laughed. 'When can I decorate it?'

'Rabbit hutch,' growled Dr Watson.

'OK Dad,' shouted Dan as he rushed off. 'I'll do it now - then I'll decorate the tree.'

He was back in ten minutes.

'That was quick,' his dad said suspiciously and he went outside to have a look.

The hutch was surprisingly clean and tidy.

'A pity it wasn't done last week,' he thought.

Dan was already at the cupboard under the stairs pulling out a large box labelled 'TREE DECORATIONS'. He emptied it in a confused pile on the floor. The lights needed untangling but that wouldn't take long. There was plenty of tinsel, at least a dozen gold and silver balls and even some chocolates.

'They must have been left over from Easter,' he said to himself.

On the packet was a picture of a long-eared rabbit. His mum came up behind him and looked over his shoulder.

'How did those get in the box? Don't hang them on the tree,' she said. 'I'll buy Christmas Tree chocolates later.'

She turned and went back into the kitchen. Dan sniffed at the packet. The smell of chocolate was tempting. He sat down and tore the end open.

'I'll just try one,' he thought.

It was delicious.

He couldn't resist another.

Within minutes, they had all gone.

He hid the empty packet at the back of the cupboard and wandered off.

The next morning he was on the landing when he heard his mum talking to a friend on the phone.

He couldn't help listening. She was talking very loudly.

'Dan will be thrilled,' she said. 'He always wanted a lop-eared rabbit. So I've bought some special chocolates. If he gives his rabbit one a day, its fur and its ears will grow really long.'

Dan suddenly felt sick.

He put his hands to his head and felt carefully. Starting to panic, he ran into the bathroom and gazed at his ears in the mirror. Were they longer?

He didn't think so - but then, he'd never taken that much notice of them before.

'Are you all right, Dan?' called his mum. 'Hurry up. Dinner's ready.'

When he came in and sat down at the table, Mrs Watson stared at him curiously.

'Are you sure you're all right? You don't look very well.'

Dan tried to eat his food but he had lost his appetite.

'I must be getting forgetful,' his mum said. 'I thought it was only a week ago you had a haircut.'

She gave him a strange look.

'It can't have been, can it?'

Dan's face turned white. He placed his hands over his ears and a tear trickled down his cheek.

'Whatever's the matter?' asked his dad anxiously. 'Shall I phone the doctor?'

Mum laughed. 'No. There's nothing to worry about. He isn't turning into a rabbit!'

But Dan still isn't sure. Every morning he hurries to the bathroom and peers anxiously into the mirror.

Thought for the day:
Sometimes things don't seem very important – but our actions always have consequences.

Something to consider:
Did you ever take something without asking? Perhaps you wished you hadn't.

This is the story of a small creature who found the world hard to understand.

Barnacle's Bad Day

Granted, Barnacle is an unusual name. But Mr and Mrs Riley thought it appropriate.

Whenever he felt hungry, the kitten would race around the house, then give a flying leap and grab something with his sharp little claws. Until his food appeared, he would stay latched on, just like a barnacle, determined not to let go. Sometimes he chose a curtain - but he preferred a bare leg or a foot.

Mr and Mrs Riley thought it was funny at first. But as Barnacle grew bigger, his claws grew longer. Gradually the screams of laughter turned to screams of pain.

One day Mr Riley, desperately dragging his leg with Barnacle attached, let out a bellow of rage.

'Get off, you stupid animal. It's agony. Get off!'

He shot out his leg violently.

The surprised cat let go, spun across the room and disappeared through the door.

Life wasn't the same after that. Not that his master and mistress were unkind to him. But he knew his fun days had gone. He must act like a grown up cat. Of course, the temptation was almost unbearable when bare toes, like tiny, plump mice, came too close. He would quickly curl up in a ball, close his eyes and pretend to sleep. If he even glanced innocently at the fish tank in the front room, they would shout at him, accusing him of wicked plans.

Then, to make matters worse, Mrs Riley disappeared mysteriously for a while. Her husband did his best to look after Barnacle but his mind seemed to be on other things. Sometimes he would forget to feed him for so long that he would despair. He would have to go hunting. It was hard work for small reward. And why was his master so cross? If Barnacle brought home a tasty mouse, he would lie on the carpet crunching its bones. It seemed good manners to leave the head and tail. Surely most people would!

He was puzzling over the problem one day, sprawled on the kitchen table licking a paw, when things suddenly became worse.

Mr Riley opened the door - and brought in his wife. In her arms was a baby. Mrs Riley looked in horror at Barnacle.

'What's that animal doing?' she cried.

The cat stared blankly at her.

'That creature on the table!' gasped Mrs Riley. 'Our poor baby. Just think of the germs!'

Before Barnacle could even wipe his whiskers he was snatched up and thrown into the garden. The door slammed. He sat gazing at it for some time.

'Why?' he wondered.

The months slipped by and Barnacle still felt confused. Mr and Mrs Riley brushed his coat daily, stroked him gently and even his meals arrived on time. But he thought nostalgically of the past - of mischievous days clowning around as a carefree kitten. The centre of attention. Laughed at and rewarded for every silly thing he did.

But nothing seemed quite the same any more.

Even the weather. One day he sat at the front window gazing out at the rain.

'I wonder if it's raining at the back of the house too.'

He sauntered through to the kitchen, went to the back door and meowed.

'All right,' called Mrs Riley. 'Have some patience. I'm coming.'

Once outside he realised his mistake. It was raining just as hard there. As the rain poured down, he meowed again and scratched desperately at the door.

'Make your mind up, will you?' snapped Mrs Riley as she flung it open. 'Either you want to go out - or you don't.'

Barnacle shook his wet fur, sighed and went back to the front room. He looked up at the fish tank.

'I could give her a present,' he thought.

He jumped onto the table. An alarmed goldfish stared across at him. Barnacle bent forward and waggled his rear end in the air, poised for a great leap.Then he changed his mind. It was too far. He dropped to the floor and wandered off.

The baby was crying upstairs.

'It's all right darling, Mummy's coming,' called Mrs Riley.

'It's not fair,' thought Barnacle sadly.

'I'm cuddly, furry and purry. The baby's ugly, noisy and bald.'

One afternoon a few days later, the table was set for tea. On a spotless white tablecloth were plates of sandwiches and cakes and all the best cups and saucers. There was also a jug of cream. Barnacle couldn't resist it. He jumped up and helped himself. It really tasted delicious. On the floor below, the baby was in her playpen, gurgling happily as she played with her toys.

Although Barnacle's head was deep in the jug, strangely - somehow - he knew something was wrong. He took one last hasty lick at the cream. Then he took his head out of the jug and stared at the crockery. He couldn't believe his eyes. Everything was gradually moving across the table.

The baby was gurgling even more happily than before. Barnacle looked down. She was clutching a corner of the tablecloth - and pulling.

Directly above her, two plates and a cup and saucer were balanced on the edge. At any moment they could fall.

Barnacle's hair stood on end.

Without thinking, he sprang from the table and raced to the kitchen.

As Barnacle came through the door with his face covered in cream, Mrs Riley was filling the teapot. She stopped and screamed at the top of her voice.

'You wicked creature! Wait till I get my hands on you!'

The cat turned and fled back to the front room. Mrs Riley was in hot pursuit. She entered the room and stopped. Suddenly she lost interest in Barnacle. She reached the playpen, caught a plate as it fell, and cuddled the baby in her arms.

'You're safe, my precious,' she whispered.

Then she glared at Barnacle.

'If I ever catch you on that table I'll . . . '

Barnacle, his hair still standing on end was trying to lick the cream from his nose. Mrs Riley started to laugh.

'How can I be cross with such a silly animal?'

Barnacle purred with delight.

Suddenly, in his imagination, he was back in the past. A carefree kitten. He stared longingly at Mrs Riley's feet.

Thought for the day:
There are times when we all feel that life is unfair.

Something to consider:
Have you ever tried to be helpful but ended up in trouble? How did it make you feel?

This is the story of Stuart, a boy whose ambition was to be an artist. But first there was an important lesson he had to learn.

Don't Touch

'Gallery of Modern Art. Exhibition Open.'

'That looks interesting,' said Stuart. 'Can we go in?'

'We might as well,' said Mum.

'Are you sure?' pleaded Dad as he searched for some money. 'It's a bit expensive, isn't it?'

Stuart couldn't wait. He was already pushing open the door to peer in.

'Wow,' he said. 'Come and look at this.'

He ran towards an enormous, strangely twisted statue. Poised on one leg with arms outstretched, the half man - half monster seemed about to leap forward, caught in a frozen moment of wild dance. The sign beside it was very clear. 'DO NOT TOUCH,' it commanded. But there was a tiny, persistent voice somewhere in the back of Stuart's mind.

'Why not?' it begged. 'Why not?'

Like thieves in the night, his fingers crept forward, longing to explore and experience the silky smoothness of the wood.

'Stuart,' hissed his mum.

He withdrew his hand quickly and hurried away. In the next room he found a gigantic, gleaming glass egg that seemed to be almost magically balanced on a metre-high needle of steel. He went over to it and gazed into the deep, swirling pools of light. He put out his hand. Again, the notice was quite clear.

'DO NOT TOUCH.'

But how could he resist?

'I don't see why I shouldn't - so I'm going to,' he muttered.

'Stuart!' snapped his dad. 'If you can't be trusted, you'll end up in real trouble,' he stormed. 'So, we're leaving now.'

They hadn't noticed a man quietly walking towards them. As he approached, he glared severely at Stuart.

'Before you go, explain why it's so important to touch my work. I'm the artist and I'd like to know.'

Stuart scratched the back of his head.

'I'm sorry. I can't help it,' he said. 'Paintings are flat. They're only to be looked at. Your sculptures are more than that, aren't they? Even a blind person could enjoy them.'

The artist smiled.

'Spoken like a true artist,' he said. 'Who knows - you might become a good one! Why not help in my studio sometimes? You could learn a lot - providing you obey the rules.'

His parents nodded eagerly.
They thought it was a very good idea!

○ ○ ○ ○ ○ ○ ○ ○ ○

Thought for the day:
It might seem that there are such a lot of laws and rules. But remember - they usually exist for a good reason.

○ ○ ○ ○ ○ ○ ○ ○ ○

Something to consider:
We need rules to protect our environment and ourselves.
If everyone going into an art exhibition touched the work it would soon be ruined, wouldn't it?

Think of some of the rules we have to obey. What dangers might there be if we ignore them?

Aunt Mo let the children stay alone on her farm. It wasn't a good idea.

Taming Billy

It could have been nice, a holiday on Highbrook Farm. But it had started badly. Annie and her brother had only been there for a few days and already wanted to go home.

Not that it was their aunt's fault. Her husband had died two years before so she had to do everything herself. The sea wasn't far away but she was always too busy to go. In any case, the weather was cold and wet.

'I'm so bored,' said Michael. 'I wish something would happen. Anything would be better than nothing.'

Annie went to the kitchen window and peered out. Through the rain she could just make out her aunt, crossing the field. The billy goat was trotting behind her like a huge pet dog.

'I hate that animal,' Annie grumbled. 'Every time we go near, he attacks us. What's so special about Aunt Mo? Why doesn't he chase her for a change?'

Michael shrugged his shoulders.

'Don't know.'

'You never know anything,' she said crossly.

Her brother suddenly pushed back his chair.

'Count to one hundred, then find me!'

Annie didn't say anything.

'I could find him with my eyes closed,' she thought.

She heard him trip over the rug in the hall. It was obvious he had gone upstairs. A floorboard in Aunt Mo's bedroom creaked loudly. Then there was silence. She wandered over to the television and switched it on.

Ten minutes later, she heard a crash and her brother swearing as he stamped back down the stairs. The kitchen door burst open.

'Watching television! Why did I bother?' he demanded.

Annie screwed up her face and pinched her nose.

'What a stink! You smell just like Aunt Mo. That's her Rose perfume!'

'Very funny!' growled Michael. 'I didn't do it on purpose. I just pressed the top and it sprayed all over the place.'

'Well you'd better wash it off before she gets back,' said Annie.

She hurriedly opened the window. A few minutes later the billy goat poked his nose in, sniffing noisily.

'I've things to attend to in town,' said their aunt next day. 'You wouldn't want to come, would you? Why not stay here and enjoy yourselves?'

'Yes Aunt, that'll be fine,' said Annie, trying to sound cheerful.

Michael made a strange snorting noise.

His sister glared at him.

'It's stopped raining so why not go to the pond?' their aunt said. 'You could make model boats from bits and pieces in the workshop.'

A short time later, she climbed into her old car. As she started the engine she called out to Annie.

'You'll be all right, won't you? Just remember to keep the gate closed.'

She waved and drove off down the lane.

Annie hurried towards the workshop. Her brother was already there, searching for anything that might float. She found what she needed and finished her boat quickly. It was hardly more than a block of wood and a paper sail. But although it was crude she felt pleased.

'I'm going to test it,' Annie said.

'Shan't be long,' said Michael. 'I'll catch up with you.'

But his sister had been at the pond for some time when he arrived. Her boat was caught in some weeds and she was trying to reach it with a stick. Michael proudly placed his in the water and gave it a push. It floated beautifully for a moment, then slowly capsized. Michael was surprised that his sister didn't laugh. She hardly seemed to notice.

'You did close the gate, didn't you?'

Michael hesitated.

'And the back door?'

'You were last out of the house, not me,' Michael retorted.

Annie thought for a moment.

'I saw a face at the bathroom window.'

'She's back early. Great,' said Michael. 'I'm hungry.'

'No, it wasn't Aunt,' said Annie. 'It was the billy goat.'

They abandoned their boats and raced back to the house. Sure enough, the back door was wide open. One of the goats was looking out. When it saw them, it gave a frightened bleat, turned and disappeared inside. Michael looked as though he might explode.

'Don't say a word,' snarled his sister. 'The whole herd must be in there. Just help me get them out.'

They tempted the animals that were downstairs with handfuls of fresh grass and leaves.

'That was simple,' laughed Michael as the last of them ran out into the yard. But when he went upstairs he found more. They were in all the bedrooms and were determined not to leave.

Annie appeared with more grass. She waved it at them while her brother pushed them from behind. They simply wouldn't move. He stamped and shouted. Then wished he hadn't.

The billy goat came to the bathroom door to see what was going on. He looked very annoyed.

'What are we going to do?' whispered Annie.

'Aunt Mo will be back soon. We've got to do something.'

'But what?' pleaded Michael as they backed hastily into their aunt's room.

At that moment a goat pushed against Annie and spat something out on the floor. It was a small bottle. Aunt Mo's Rose perfume. Annie picked it up and sniffed thoughtfully. She screwed up her nose.

'Revolting - but the goats seem to like it!' she said.

Suddenly she knew what to do. She pointed the bottle at her brother and sprayed. Michael nearly choked.

'What a stink! Why did you do that?' he yelled.

But instead of answering, she turned it on herself.

'Don't make such a fuss,' she said impatiently. 'Just follow me.'

She crept cautiously past the bathroom. Billy was standing there. He lowered his head menacingly. Would he charge? They hurried past quickly. Half way down the stairs, they looked back. He had come out onto the landing, sniffing the air. Slowly, he approached the stairs. Then other goats appeared.

'They're following us. I don't believe it,' whispered Michael.

An hour later, when Aunt Mo arrived home, the children were watching television.

'The house is in a terrible mess. There's mud everywhere,' she thought.

'Never mind. As long as they've enjoyed themselves.'

Then her nose started to twitch!

'Michael, have you been using my perfume? I'm surprised but I don't really mind. It's nice, isn't it?'

Annie looked at her brother, grinned, then started to giggle. He scowled at her. Then he started to laugh too.

The next day was sunny. They all went to the beach and had a wonderful time.

○ ○ ○ ○ ○ ○ ○ ○ ○

Thought for the day:
When you walk through the countryside, always close the gates. Animals need to be kept safe.

○ ○ ○ ○ ○ ○ ○ ○ ○

Something to consider:
Aunt Mo hadn't thought much about safety on her farm. What dangers did the children face when left alone?

Fiona simply wanted some fun.
She didn't think of the consequences of her actions.

The Crash

Peter was sprawled on the sofa watching TV. If he hadn't been hungrily scrunching a packet of beef and mustard crisps he might have noticed his sister creeping up behind him.

Fiona slowly raised a thin metal tube to her mouth, aimed it at his ear - and puffed. He felt the blast of air and swung round sharply.

'Don't!' he snapped.

She laughed as he shoved her away.

'Think about what you're doing,' he said irritably. 'If you poke someone in the ear it can be serious.'

His sister wandered off and he settled down to watch his favourite programme.

Half an hour later she returned.

'Look Pete,' she said. 'I've found one for you too.'

She held out another tube. He took it from her and glanced at it.

'So what do I do with it?' he asked.

He didn't sound very enthusiastic.

'I found these dried peas in the kitchen,' said Fiona. 'I bet Mum doesn't need them.'

Her brother stretched out his hand.

'O.K. Give me one, then,' he said.

He placed it in the tube, took a deep breath, aimed and blew. The pea shot across the room.

'Right on the nose,' Peter cackled. 'Perfect shot.'

Granddad, in the photo on the mantelpiece, glared ferociously at him.

'Too easy,' said his sister. 'How about a moving target?'

'O.K. Let's go outside. If you're so clever, let's see if you can hit a bird.'

They ran into the garden, lay down in the grass and waited. But no birds appeared.

'Too much traffic,' said Fiona. 'The birds are scared of the noise.'

'How about cars then?' said Peter. 'I bet you can't hit one!'

'Just watch,' laughed his sister.

A large red car was passing. She aimed carefully . . . took a very deep breath . . . and blew.

'Perfect shot,' she said.

'How do you know? Her brother sniggered. I'd say you missed by miles!'

'A perfect shot,' insisted Fiona. 'It hit the windscreen. The driver almost leaped out of his seat! Didn't you see?'

The next moment there was a squeal of brakes. There was the sound of metal crumpling and glass shattering.

The children ran out onto the pavement and stared in horror. A short way down the road, the red car had crashed into a lamp post. After a few minutes the door slowly opened and a man staggered out. He looked shocked and dazed.

Peter and Fiona glanced at each other, then turned and rushed into the house. A police siren was wailing in the distance. They went into the front room and sat in stony silence.

Dad put down his paper.

'What have you two been doing?' he asked suspiciously.

Fiona felt her hands trembling as she pretended to study the pattern on the carpet.

'Nothing,' she said.

Peter shrugged his shoulders.

'Anything on television?' he asked.

'Are you all right Fiona?' asked Mum next morning. 'You don't look very well.'

'I'm fine,' Fiona said quietly.

But of course, she wasn't. She couldn't stop thinking about the crash. All night she had tossed and turned and worried.

'Has the driver been hurt?' she thought. 'What will happen to me? I've done a terrible thing.'

Dad came into the kitchen.

'There was a car crash yesterday,' he said. 'Just down the road from here. It was on the news. The idiot who caused it needs her brains tested.'

'Why? What happened?' her mum asked.

Fiona's heart was pounding. She got up from her chair and hurried from the room. Five minutes later, Peter found her in her bedroom. She had obviously been crying.

'It's OK. You weren't to blame,' he said. 'Dad says a woman suddenly stepped into the road. The car had to swerve to miss her.'

Fiona thought hard for some time.

'It could have been my fault though . . . couldn't it?' she said.

Thought for the day:
We must always think before we act.

Something to consider:
Could Fiona's pea shooter have caused the accident? What do you think?

Sam was brilliant at football. He dreamt that one day his talent might bring fame and fortune. But in one reckless moment he risked everything. Even his life.

The Boy Who Danced

The ball hardly left Sam's feet as he danced his way across the field, weaving his way past the other boys.

A lightning sprint, a leap, a spin and a skip . . . Then - hardly pausing to aim - he kicked the ball. It all seemed so easy. It happened with such speed that for a second, no one could believe what had happened.

'Goal . . . goal!' shrieked his friends.

'I've never seen anything like it,' said Mr Harper. He blew the whistle. 'Practice over,' he shouted.

Sam flung his bag on his back and wandered towards home, whistling quietly to himself. His friend Tim passed on his bike.

'See you down the club,' he called.

There were burgers, chips and beans for tea. Sam downed the lot, smacking his lips noisily.

'Do you have to gobble your food?' pleaded his mum. 'You've the manners of a wart hog.'

Sam grinned as he pushed back his chair.

'I'm meeting Tim down the club in five minutes.'

'You're not,' she snapped. 'What about homework?'

'There's hardly any tonight. I'll do it later.'

'Just make sure you do,' she said.

But he was already out of the back door and half way to the garden shed. He heaved out his bike and, moments later, was racing down the street.

The 'Club' was on the Woodbridge Estate. It was only a ramshackle corrugated iron building but it was a great place to meet, particularly on cold winter nights. When Sam arrived, Tim was sitting outside on his bike.

'We forgot, didn't we? It's closed. All the windows got smashed last week!' Sam swore under his breath. 'So what do we do?'

'The gang might be over at the cutting,' Tim suggested.

By the time they got there, it was almost dusk. They followed the path through the allotments, swung their bikes under the twisted remains of a fence and were there. The railway cutting was a favourite haunt of the gang, where they could dare each other to ride down the frighteningly sheer slope to the track below.

The gang were nowhere to be seen.

'So what now?' asked Tim.

Sam shrugged his shoulders.

'Can't be too long. I've loads of homework tonight.'

'O.K. Now we're here, we'll have one go each. Unless we're quick it'll be too dark . . . Me first.'

Perched on the edge of the precipice, Tim sat on his bike, testing the brakes. Then he counted.

Three . . . Two . . . One!

He pushed himself off.

'Last flight of Concorde!' he yelled.

With stomach in mouth, he plummeted down the slope. Suddenly, as the ground levelled out, he swerved sideways. The railway line hurtled towards him. He wobbled, slammed on the brakes . . . and slid to a halt.

'Made it . . . just!' he laughed.

He glanced up and waved. Sam waved back. He was ready to go. He took a deep breath . . . grasped the handlebars tightly . . . pushed himself forward . . . and was away.

Down he went. Down and down.

It was difficult to hear with the wind rushing past his face. But he was aware of his friend shouting. And a moment later the words became clear.

'A train! A train!'

'What's he talking about? The line's been closed for years.'

But even as a hundred thoughts flashed through his mind, he pulled desperately on the brakes. The bike swung from side to side as he struggled to control it.

He failed. The front wheel twisted violently, the bike swerved sideways and Sam tumbled headlong towards the track. He struck his head on the ground and lay still.

A diesel freight train thundered past with a deafening roar. His friend turned his back and covered his ears with his hands. The blast of wind almost knocked him over.

A week later Sam was back at school.

'A lump on the head but no broken bones,' said Mr Harper. 'Amazing! You could easily have been killed!'

Sam stuck his hands in his pockets and nodded gloomily. He was close to tears.

'Cheer up,' said his teacher. 'You've been very lucky.'

'You know what football means to me?' Sam asked. 'I've been to the field to practise. My footwork is as good as ever – but you know what happens when I kick the ball? I'm rubbish. A two year old could do better.'

Mr Harper thought for a moment.

'A bang on the head can do strange things,' he said. 'Give it time. Determination can work wonders. But whatever happens, you've still got a wonderful gift - your footwork. Ever tried dancing?'

Sam laughed bitterly.

'You have to be joking. That's for girls.'

○ ○ ○ ○ ○ ○ ○ ○ ○

Thought for the day:

Perhaps, with patience and hard work, Sam's football skills returned.

But there are times when we all experience disappointments.There's an old saying that's worth remembering . . . When one door closes, another opens.

○ ○ ○ ○ ○ ○ ○ ○ ○

What's your opinion?

Was Sam right about dancing? Is it just for girls?

The village where Mark and Paul lived was split in two by the main road to London. The traffic was so heavy and moved at such speed that it was almost impossible to cross.

Not surprisingly, there had been many accidents.

Owning Up

Mrs Davey was about to close the front door. She paused for a moment.

'I'll only be an hour,' she called. 'Mark, don't forget. Look after your brother, and whatever you do, keep right away from the main road.'

'O.K., Mum,' he answered. 'We're meeting the gang. I expect we'll go to the woods.'

The door slammed as Paul ran down the stairs.

'I'll just get some money,' said his brother.

Paul was puzzled.

'We don't need money, do we?'

'How do I know?' said Mark sharply. 'Depends on the gang.'

Ten minutes later, they found Carl, Sid and Pete staring hungrily at the chip shop. It was closed.

'Where are we going then?' asked Mark. 'The woods?'

The gang looked blankly at him. Pete shrugged his shoulders.

'Don't care,' he said. 'But I'm starving. Got any money? We could get some coke and crisps or something.'

Carl grinned and smacked his lips.

'Great idea,' he said. 'What are we waiting for?'

Mark pulled a handful of coins from his pocket and counted them. His brother looked anxiously at the traffic thundering past - and the shop on the other side of the road.

'Come on then,' said Sid.

They all waited on the kerb, buffeted by the wind from gigantic lorries. They waited and waited.

'We must time it right,' Pete shouted.

'Ready? . . . Now!'

Instantly, they rushed to the other side.

'That was close,' laughed Sid breathlessly.

'Where's my little brother gone?' Mark muttered.

He looked round. There he was, still on the kerb. He looked frightened. Mark sighed crossly.

'Stay there,' he yelled. 'Shan't be a minute.'

He turned and followed the gang into the shop.

When they came out, Paul was still standing where they'd left him. Mark grinned and waved a carrier bag in the air.

The traffic seemed even worse. Minutes ticked by and there was no gap.

'Ready?' yelled Pete suddenly . . . 'Now!'

They dived across the road. There was a scream of brakes and smoke billowed up from the tyres of a lorry. The boys glanced up at the white faced driver, screamed with laughter and ran on.

'We're going to the woods for a feast,' Mark said to his brother.

Paul stared at him crossly.

'I'm going home.'

'O.K. Suit yourself,' said Mark.

He put his hand in the bag and pulled out a packet of sweets.

'Have these. I'll see you later.'

Paul was watching a video when his mum came home.

'Everything's all right?' she asked. 'Where's your brother?'

'Down the woods,' Paul said.

'What's this?' Mum asked picking up the empty sweet packet from the floor. 'I told you not to. You've been to the shop - across the road. Haven't you?' she screamed.

The door opened and Mark walked in.

'Sorry Mum,' Paul mumbled.

His brother didn't say anything. He hurried upstairs to his room. He felt scared. Even with the door closed, he could hear his mum shouting.

Thought for the day:

Always think for yourself. Don't blindly follow others.

Something to consider:

Paul could so easily have said that he wasn't to blame - that it was his brother who had crossed the main road.

Should he have told his mother what really happened?

As Harry and Ben found out, there was a good reason for obeying their mum!

Following the Crowd

'Where are you two going?' called Mum as Harry and Ben left the house.

'Meeting some of the gang,' yelled Harry. 'Shan't be long.'

'Well, don't you dare go near the farm. You've caused enough trouble up there already!'

The boys may have heard her. She couldn't be sure. They were already running off down the lane. The gang weren't far away. There they were, six bored-looking boys, sitting on a wall. As the two brothers approached, the 'gang' got to their feet.

'You've taken your time. We were about to go,' said Pete, a tall boy who always liked to take charge.

'Come on then - let's get up to the farm.'

Ben looked doubtful.

'The farmer said he'd call the police if he caught us again.'

'Baby,' sneered his brother.

'Go home to mummy if you like,' added Pete. 'We don't care.'

He turned and walked quickly off along the farm track. The others hurried after him. Ben stayed close to his brother. He didn't look very happy. Harry glared at him.

'I'm warning you. If you tell Mum, you're dead.'

They stopped talking and peered round furtively. They were getting close to the farm.

'Any sign of him?' whispered one of the boys.

'No, it's safe. His car isn't there,' said another.

'O.K.' shouted Pete. 'Let's go!'

A ladder was leaning against the barn. Pete charged through a patch of oozing mud to reach it. He was at the top in seconds.

'DANGER. KEEP OFF THE ROOF.'

He ignored the sign.

'Find me!' he yelled.

He waved his arms in the air, poked his tongue out, then ran across the roof and disappeared. The gang ran round the corner and into the huge barn, hooting with excitement. As usual, it was stacked with bales of hay and straw.

'He's in here somewhere,' shouted Harry.

With loud war cries they rushed forward, some diving into narrow tunnels in the straw.

Ben could see the hole in the roof that Pete had jumped through. The bales at that end were piled very high. Three of the boys were pulling themselves towards the top.

'They can search all day if they like. I don't care,' thought Ben.

He found a gap well away from them and pushed his way in.

'A tomb in ancient Egypt,' he whispered to himself.

It was very dark. Occasionally, as he squeezed further in, he heard muffled shouts. Then, in the distance, he heard another sound.

A tractor. . . the farmer had returned.

The others heard it too. Pete sprang out.

'Owen's coming. Run for it!'

Immediately, scared faces appeared between the bales.

'Don't hang about, you lot. Follow me!'

They rushed from the barn, but too late. The noise of the tractor engine was getting louder. They were trapped.

'Not that way!' yelled Pete. 'Get over here, behind the shed.'

The roar of the engine was now deafening.

'Keep your heads down or he'll see you.'

They couldn't hear Pete's command. But it hardly mattered. No one dared move a muscle for fear of discovery.

Harry, crouched at the far end of the wall, stared thoughtfully at the back of six heads.

'Six? That can't be right. Someone's missing.' He started to feel anxious. Ben. Where was he?

He peered cautiously round the corner. The exhaust was belching fumes as the tractor, fitted with a row of deadly steel prongs, drove quickly into the barn. Terrified, Harry ran in after it.

'Stop!' he shrieked. 'Stop!'

He was too late.

Mr Owen saw him out of the corner of his eye. Surprised, he turned to look at Harry, but couldn't hear.

The tractor rolled forward too fast. The prongs plunged into the highest tower of bales and they toppled sideways.

Bewildered, the rest of the gang came up behind Harry.

The tractor engine fell silent.

'What's wrong?' asked Pete.

The farmer clambered down. He was seething with anger.

'Yes. Just what is wrong? I've warned you boys before. Keep off my farm or I'll call the police. Someone will get killed one of these days.'

Harry burst into tears as he stared at the prongs and the tumbled bales.

'My brother,' he blurted. 'He was in there.'

In hushed silence everyone rushed forward. They pushed and pulled but the bales were too heavy. Even the farmer couldn't shift them.

'It's no good. The fire brigade are the people we need.'

He hesitated for a moment.

'And an ambulance,' he added.

He pulled a mobile phone from his pocket. The boys stood in hushed silence.

'What's wrong? Is everything O.K?'

It was a familiar voice. Everyone turned to look. A small boy was standing in the barn entrance, covered in mud. Harry wiped away his tears with the back of his hand.

'I thought you were dead,' he gasped.

'Me? No I'm not dead,' said Ben. 'I got out of the barn through a hole in the wall. But Mr Owen - do you know how mucky it is back there? I stink. Mum will kill me when I get home.'

Thought for the day:
Wherever there is machinery there is danger!

Something to consider:
Harry's brother knew it was wrong to go to the farm. So why do you think he still went?

This is a true story. Harry was an inventor. Without his clear thinking, the American space programme might have failed.

The Challenge

The journey wasn't long but it was exciting. Robert had hardly ever been on a train before - and certainly never on his own.

His mother had agreed, but at the last moment she nearly changed her mind.

'Are you sure you'll be all right? I really should come with you,' she said anxiously.

'Don't worry,' said Robert. 'Uncle will meet me at Monkton Station. I'll be fine.'

He hadn't seen Uncle Harry for many years, but when he stepped off the train he recognised the man easily enough. He was tall and thin with a shock of white hair. Although he wasn't young, his eyes were alert and twinkling.

'I don't know why you're looking so excited,' he said. 'A whole weekend to fill! What are we going to do?'

'Mum says you worked on the first rocket to reach the moon. I want to be an inventor - like you. You can teach me.'

Uncle Harry chuckled as they got into his dilapidated old car.

'Inventing! New ideas to change the world! I can't teach you that. All I can do is set you a little challenge, just to help!'

'What sort of challenge?' Robert asked.

His uncle didn't answer. He just smiled.

When they pulled up in the drive, the ramshackle house looked much as he remembered it, except that the gardens were more overgrown. They had to struggle through waist-high grass, brambles and nettles simply to reach the front door. Inside, his uncle helped him climb over piles of books in the hall and squeeze past a gleaming but ancient motorcycle. Every space was piled high with so many things. It was like the biggest, most chaotic junk shop Robert could possibly imagine!

At last they got to the stairs.

'Go up carefully,' his uncle warned. 'Don't trip over anything. You could have a nasty fall. Here's your bedroom,' he said when they reached the landing. 'Sorry there isn't more space.'

'Is this the challenge?' laughed Robert.

There were so many mysterious machines hidden under thick layers of dust that it was almost impossible to reach the bed.

Downstairs again, he followed his uncle along another cluttered corridor. Suddenly Robert stopped. On one of the doors was a notice.

It said, 'DO NOT ENTER.'

'What's in there?' he asked. 'Could that be the challenge?' he thought.

His uncle gave him a serious look.

'Never go in there without me. Dangerous.'

Robert was dying to know what dark secret might lie within, but his uncle had already flung open another door.

'This,' he said, 'is my computer room. I'm not sure how many are there. I did try to count them once.'

Robert stood in the doorway and looked in. Some computers were on tables but most were stacked untidily around the walls.

'So what do you need them for?'

'I take them to pieces - as an inventor, odd bits often come in useful - if I can remember where I've put them.' Then he thought for a moment. 'After tea we'll go into the garden.'

'But it'll be too dark to see anything,' Robert protested. 'I'd rather get on with the challenge.'

Robert was still eating a piece of cake when Harry suddenly got up from the table.

'Come on. We'll go outside now and take a photo.'

He went over to the sideboard and picked up an old, cheap looking camera. He studied it for a moment.

'We're in luck,' he said. 'There's one picture left on the film.'

'But uncle, it hasn't a flash. How can we take a photo of anything outside? It's too dark.'

His uncle grinned.

'No, it isn't,' he said. 'Come on. You're in charge of the camera.'

They struggled back down the corridor and out into the night.

'This is a silly challenge,' laughed Robert. 'I can't see anything.'

'Of course you can,' said Harry. 'It's bigger than anything you can possibly imagine!'

His nephew felt bewildered for a moment.

Then he understood. He looked up at the sky. It was breathtaking. In all directions were thousands of twinkling stars.

'I've set the shutter to stay open. Just place the camera on the ground, press the button on the side and we'll leave it. Let's look for shooting stars while we wait.'

'My neck's starting to ache,' groaned Robert after a quarter of an hour.

'But it was worth it. I've seen three already!'

'It's surprising what you discover if you look hard enough,' said his uncle.

'Let's take the camera in now. We'll see what we've got.'

Robert hesitated in front of the door. The notice was very clear.

'DO NOT ENTER.'

'Go on in,' urged Harry. 'But don't touch anything yet.'

There was a mysterious red glow in the small room. On some shelves was an assortment of bottles. In the centre of the room there was some equipment on a table, with some trays and jugs.

Robert felt disappointed. It didn't look very exciting.

'It's my dark room,' said Harry proudly. 'Do be careful. Chemicals are dangerous - but with a bit of patience we'll soon have our picture of the stars.'

He opened the camera. Robert helped mix some chemicals. Then his uncle dropped the film in.

'That's a good start,' he said. 'I'll show you what to do next.'

They worked busily for the next half hour.

At last they had finished. Harry held up the photo.

'Just look at that!' he said. Beautiful, isn't it?'

Robert studied the picture silently for some time. He didn't understand.

' What went wrong?' he said. 'Those aren't stars. Just lots of curving lines.'

'Learn to think clearly,' said his uncle. 'That's your challenge.'

Thought for the day:

Inventors are people like you and me, always learning - and searching for new ideas that we hope will improve our world.

Something to consider:

Robert's photo didn't turn out as he expected. Can you think of a reason why?

This is the true story of a boy who lived 200 years ago.
He was clever, ambitious - and he was determined.

Even the Greatest

A boy stood on the deck of a ship. He was gazing sadly at the coastline of France getting fainter every moment. He turned to his father.

'Did we really have to leave?' he asked.

'Yes Isi,' his dad said. 'I've had enough of revolution and war. From now on, England will be home.'

A fishing boat was passing, its sails billowing in the wind as it sped back to Calais. The men on board waved as they hauled in their nets.

'Au revoir,' Isi shouted. Then he looked to the north, to the distant cliffs of Dover. 'What's England like?' he asked.

'For an engineer like me? Paradise!' his dad said. 'A land full of energy, new inventions, new ideas.'

'But what shall we do there?' pleaded Isi. 'Where shall we live?'

His father chuckled.

'One thing at a time! First we go to Scotland to see a new ship launched. A ship made of iron.'

His son looked puzzled.

'That's impossible. Iron's too heavy. It'll sink like a stone!'

'Impossible? Don't be so sure,' said his dad.

'But wood floats and iron doesn't,' the boy protested.

His father shook his head impatiently.

'You want to be an engineer, don't you?'

'Yes. More than anything in the world.'

'Then you will be,' said his dad. 'In fact you could even be the greatest if you work hard - and never use the word impossible again!'

It was 24 years later.

The boy had grown into a man. Isi had worked hard and followed his dream. He had become an engineer. One of the best.

In fact, his bridges, railways and boats were so amazing that people stopped and pointed when they saw him.

'Look,' they gasped. 'There's the famous Mr Isambard Brunel.'

Isi, smartly dressed in a black suit and coat, doffed his hat as he leaned out of the carriage window.

'A perfect day for the launch,' he thought.

He could see the masts of his wonderful new ship towering over the rooftops of Bristol. Everywhere, excited people were hurrying to the docks through streets hung with flags.

'This way sir, please.'

A man bowed and beckoned him to follow. Mr Brunel strode proudly forward.

'A day we'll never forget!' he shouted.

'The Great Britain - the fastest and most powerful iron ship in the world!'

Hundreds of policemen were swept along by the enormous crowd surging after him.

Half an hour later, after a rousing speech, he was bursting with excitement. His magnificent ship was floating at last. It slowly gathered speed between the narrow dock walls on its short journey to the sea. Bands marched as they played and church bells rang out across the city. The cheering of the crowd became a deafening roar.

Isi looked at his watch.

'Just ten minutes more,' he thought. 'Then full steam ahead. I've done it! I'm the greatest engineer the world has ever seen.'

But gradually the cheers were changing to gasps of dismay. The crowd fell silent. The only sound, the laughter of a small boy.

'Look,' he hooted. 'Brunel forgot his tape measure. The ship's too big. It's stuck!'

It was true.

The greatest engineer in the world had made a very silly mistake. The ship was too big. It was going nowhere. It was firmly wedged in the dock!

His face turned purple.

Trembling, he turned and hurried hastily away. A sullen crowd followed, angrily tearing down flags as they went.

The party was over.

Thought for the day:

We all make mistakes – no matter how clever we are. But remember, if things go wrong, don't give up - try, try, try again!

Something to consider:

How Brunel made such a blunder we'll probably never know. But it wasn't a disaster. After a whole year of struggling, The Great Britain did finally reach the sea. She proved to be a wonderful ship, carrying passengers and cargo for thousands of miles around the world. Even today you can enjoy seeing her - back in the dock where she was built, in Bristol.

Perhaps you can find out more about The Great Britain - and Brunel's other great achievements too.

The boy in this story may not have been entirely honest. Was he as clever as he claimed? We don't know. But I'm sure you'll agree, he was definitely good at boasting!

The Unstoppable

When Mr Harris suggested a Technology competition, he knew it would cause excitement. 'What's the prize?' Martin Stokes called from the back of the class.

Mr Harris pulled open the drawer of his desk and produced an envelope.

'Book vouchers,' he said, '. . . and a free family weekend at Alton Towers.'

Everyone gasped.

'Sir! What do we have to do?' pleaded Lucy Palmer.

'Don't bother asking,' Martin Stokes sniggered. 'You couldn't even win a game of Snap.'

'Anyone could win,' said their teacher. 'Of course it'll take skill - but also determination and hard work.'

'But what do we have to do?' repeated Lucy.

'Design and make a coin sorting machine. It must be entirely your own work. No help from anyone. You have one week.'

'I'm going to be an engineer like my father,' bragged Martin. 'None of you stand a chance!'

Lucy would prove him wrong. She was determined.

She rushed home, her head already buzzing with plans. Within hours, her bedroom floor was strewn with empty boxes and tubes and a pile of wood, plastic, and card. As the days went by she worked feverishly, sometimes long after her bedtime.

Every night she covered her mysterious machine with a blanket. 'TOP SECRET' said the notice on the door.

Excitement mounted as Saturday – and the 'Technology Challenge' - drew closer. On Friday evening when Lucy was watching television, her mum crept upstairs for a sneaking peep. She dashed down again.

'Lucy - I really didn't mean to . . .'

Lucy looked shocked.

'What?' she gasped. 'After all my work . . . you've broken it?'

Mum grinned.

'No! But curiosity got the better of me. I know it was a secret - but I've seen your invention. I think it's amazing.'

The next day, the children carried their machines into school.

'Place them on the tables,' said Mr Harris.

'The competition starts in ten minutes. In the meantime, there are refreshments in the corner. Sweets and cakes. Help yourselves!'

There was an instant stampede!

'Jelly babies,' said Lucy. 'Delicious.'

She picked up a handful.

'Attention everyone, it's time to start the competition,' shouted Mr Harris.

'But "Know-all Martin" isn't here!' someone whispered.

'Where is he?'

At that moment the door burst open and in he came with his dad. They were staggering under the weight of a gigantic machine made of gleaming metal and glass. 'THE GREAT UNSTOPPABLE,' was painted in immaculate lettering on the side. They struggled to a table and placed it down.

Mr Harris walked over.

'Well done, Martin,' he said. 'You must have worked hard.'

Martin looked uncomfortable for a moment. Then he beamed.

'Yes,' he mumbled. 'All my own work.'

Lucy and a crowd of her friends gathered round to look.

'Wow,' someone said. 'Did you really make it - all on your own?'

'Yes. It was easy,' he said.

Lucy stared at it. She didn't know what to say.

'Careful with those jelly babies,' whispered a mischievous little voice. 'They're very sticky, aren't they? One could fall in the machine.'

'It's time to begin,' called Mr Harris. 'The machine that sorts the most coins in five minutes is the winner. Are you ready? . . . Start!'

Brothers, sisters, parents and friends shouted and screamed. Machines clattered and clanked, wheels turned and levers rose and fell - and Mr Harris watched the seconds tick away on his watch.

'Stop,' he ordered suddenly.

There was a hushed silence as their teacher checked the results. Then he walked to the centre of the room.

'The winner,' he announced, ' . . . an incredible machine . . . that counted more than any other . . . '

Lucy could hardly bear to listen. She held her breath.

'The winner is . . . the Unstoppable! Congratulations, Martin!'

There was polite clapping as Martin posed proudly for the cameras.

'All his own work? I don't believe it!' Lucy muttered. 'Why did I bother?'

She felt bitterly disappointed.

When she was half way home she remembered the jelly babies. She pulled one out of her pocket. It really was very sticky.

'I could easily have dropped it in,' she thought. 'Accidentally, of course!'

She imagined Martin's fury and smiled. She knew that in a funny sort of way she had won after all!

Thought for the day:

In the real world, we can't all be 'best', can we? But what do we mean by best anyway?

What's your opinion?

Lucy was so sure Martin had cheated. Perhaps she should have stopped him winning. What do you think? It would have been easy, wouldn't it?

This is the story of Bruno, a very special dog.

The Last Bark

If you ever visit London, take an evening boat trip on the Thames. As the sun sets and you approach Westminster Bridge you'll enjoy a beautiful scene - the towers of the Houses of Parliament reflected in the river.

From the outside it all looks so peaceful.

Don't be deceived.

Inside, as members discuss important things, they sometimes rant and rave and jeer and shout. There was a time when things were even worse. But that was before Bruno arrived. After many months of training, he was ready for a very important task. He was the new guide dog for a blind politician. We'll call him 'Mr B.'

On his first day in Parliament, Bruno strutted proudly across the polished marble floors, leading his master to the debating chamber.

He felt very important, making sure that Mr B safely reached his seat. Then he lay down at his feet to sleep until needed.

For a while he was aware of voices talking as he dreamed of juicy chunks of meat. But gradually the voices became louder. Bruno woke up. He anxiously opened one eye.

The Members of Parliament were shaking their fists and arguing angrily. The Speaker of the House leaped to his feet.

He took a deep breath and bellowed, 'Order! Order!' His face turned a frightening shade of purple.

The dog opened his other eye. With his chin still on the floor, he looked round at the sea of hostile faces. Shouting furiously, the Prime Minister flung some papers in the air. Poor Bruno panicked.

He sprang forward.

Standing in the middle of the chamber, he growled. Then he raised his head high, opened his mouth and barked. He barked and barked and barked. Gradually the Members of Parliament stopped their noise.

'Come here boy,' said a calm voice.

The dog turned, trotted back to his master, lay down again and closed his eyes. It was quiet enough to hear a fairy sneeze.

The Prime Minister gazed at Bruno thoughtfully.

'Thank you,' he said. 'This wise young animal has told us how to behave.'

Mr B leaned forward and patted his dog gently.

'Well done,' he whispered.

At the end of the day, when the debating was over, Bruno got to his feet, stretched and yawned, then guided his master from the chamber.

This time, he didn't mind the noise. With tail wagging, he marched through the door as everyone stood to clap and cheer.

Even now, when members debate important things, they sometimes forget. They sneer and snarl and shout.

The noise can be unbelievable.

If Bruno hears the Speaker of the House bellow 'Order . . . Order!' he's tempted, once again, to remind them with a helpful bark.

But instead he simply shuts his eyes and thinks his own wise thoughts.

○ ○ ○ ○ ○ ○ ○ ○ ○

Thought for the day:
Humans can be clever and wise but we sometimes behave very badly.

○ ○ ○ ○ ○ ○ ○ ○ ○

Something to consider:
Do other people make you angry?
Do you lose your temper? If so, what happens?